# PIRATES
## AND PRIVATEERS

# PIRATES
## AND PRIVATEERS

### A SWASHBUCKLING COMPENDIUM
### OF SEAFARING SCOUNDRELS

Charlotte Montague

CHARTWELL
BOOKS

# CONTENTS

## INTRODUCTION
···· 6 ····

 PIRATES

## THE PIRATE CODE
···· 84 ····

## PIRATE PUNISHMENTS
···· 86 ····

# PRIVATEERS

# WOMEN PIRATES

## MODERN PIRACY

## PIRATES IN POPULAR CULTURE

## GLOSSARY

## INDEX

# INTRODUCTION

The image of the pirate is one that still excites and fascinates us today. We all recognize the familiar figure of the man with the jaunty tricorne hat, the eyepatch, and the flamboyant, tattered clothes, burying his treasure chest on a remote island, flying the Jolly Roger aboard his outlaw ship, or drawing his cutlass with a bloodcurdling yell. He remains part of our popular culture, whether in classic adventure stories such as Robert Louis Stevenson's *Treasure Island*, popular contemporary films like *Pirates of the Caribbean*, or simply as a costume in a child's dressing-up box. But what is the reality behind the myth? And why does this largely historical icon still carry such resonance in the modern world?

## ANCIENT SEA CRIME

Piracy has existed since ancient times. The name comes from the Latin *pirata* and from the Greek *piera* meaning 'to attempt', and described the sea robbers that preyed on ships and coastal settlements around the Mediterranean and beyond. In Greek and Roman civilization, the Thracians, Tyrsenians, Illyrians and Phoenicians – who specialized in kidnapping children to sell as slaves – were all known and feared as pirates. Julius Caesar himself was captured by Sicilian pirates, who demanded a ransom of 25 gold talents. Caesar thought he was worth more, and

demanded they raise the ransom to 50, which his supporters duly paid. However, once Caesar was freed, he took his revenge: he pursued the pirates, captured them, and had them all put to death.

During the Dark Ages, from the fall of the Roman Empire to the medieval period, European civilization was under attack from marauding bands of pirates everywhere. From the East Germanic tribes came the Goths; from Scandinavia, the Vikings, ruthless warriors who raided all the great cities of Europe. These scavengers of the sea were joined by Narentines from Croatia, Ushkuiniks from Russia, and Maniots from Greece, as well as Muslims, Slavs and Celts from different tribes across the continent. In India and the Far East, piracy was also thriving, threatening the stability of empires and dynasties there. But it was not until the 16th century that piracy reached its apogee, as the colonial powers of Europe began to underwrite the brigands, in an attempt to gain control of the New World.

## THE 'GOLDEN AGE' OF PIRACY

Piracy has always been an attractive option to those who find themselves at the bottom of the social and economic heap. As Black Bart, the most successful pirate of the 17th century, put it, 'in honest service there is thin commons, low wages,

and hard labour. In this (the life of piracy), plenty and satiety, pleasure and ease, liberty and power.' He was well aware of the risk of being hanged, which was the standard punishment for piracy at the time, but he took the view that it was a risk worth taking: 'And who would not balance creditor on this side, when all the hazard that is run for it, at worst is only a sour look or two at choking? No, a merry life and a short one shall be my motto.'

The common criminal, on the run from the long arm of the law, was a typical recruit to piracy. Such a man was l'Olonnais, one of the most bloodthirsty pirates in history; another was the ex-slave Black Caesar, who ran a rebel colony on the Florida Keys. There were also many who defected from the British Navy, fed up with the poor pay and conditions, and used their maritime skills in the cause of robbery instead. Black Bart, quoted above, was one of these, as was another extremely successful pirate of the period, Henry Avery.

But from the 16th century on, a new breed of pirate began to swell the ranks of the rough-and-ready sea robbers. These men were often from well-educated merchant families – some of them even noblemen with connections to the monarchy – who owned their own ships and directed their own, often much more professional, operations. They, and their ships, became known as 'privateers'.

## LICENSED TO ROB

A privateer was the owner of a ship who had obtained a 'letter of marque' from the state authorizing the bearer to attack enemy shipping. The idea was that, in times of warfare, governments could commandeer private ships to help fight their battles at sea, at little or no cost to themselves. As part of the deal, the privateer might be allowed to keep his 'prizes' – captured enemy ships and cargo – or he might be required to bring them back to the authorities and split the profits. Theoretically, this system worked well for both the privateer and his sponsors: neither

had any real responsibilities to each other, and each could act independently.

In practice, however, the privateer system turned out to be nothing more than a state-supported form of piracy. The privateers were very much their own bosses, and would attack and capture other ships – whether enemy or not – as they thought fit. Their letters of marque effectively gave them *carte blanche* to do as they pleased. Communication was slow in those days, and news could take months to travel, so that the privateers could get away with murder. Moreover, in many instances, there was no formal war going on, yet attacks were made indiscriminately, both at sea and on land. These attacks were illegal, yet the British authorities turned a blind eye to them because in a general way, it was in their interests to undermine the power of the Spanish and the French in the New World, where the battle for supremacy was raging.

In a sense, during this period of history, all the major European powers were involved in robbery on a grand scale, squabbling over the spoils of the territories they had claimed in the New World; and the privateers simply became pawns in their game, making out – quite literally – like bandits, while the kings and queens of Europe plundered and pillaged their way through the Americas, claiming them for their own.

## RICH PICKINGS

Naturally enough, the more astute privateers took advantage of the unstable political situation to make a fortune for themselves. The Welshman Henry Morgan, for example, who became one of the most successful privateers in history, made a series of ferocious attacks on coastal cities, towns and settlements in South America, amassing enormous personal wealth in the process. It is said that he had a letter of marque for each and every attack he made, though of course, many of these must have been spurious. Occasionally, Morgan went too far, and in one case was arrested – for

the ransacking of Panama – but his punishment amounted to no more than a rap on the knuckles, and eventually he died a very rich man, rather than being hung as a thief. For although the authorities made a great show of punishing piracy, hanging the miscreants and leaving their bodies out to rot as a warning to would-be lawbreakers – as happened to Blackbeard, Calico Jack, Charles Vane and others - when it suited their purposes, they were quite happy to let the more illustrious freebooters carry on their ugly trade around the globe.

And there were plenty of prestigious figures involved in the nefarious world of piracy and privateering: Sir Walter Raleigh, Sir Francis Drake and Sir Christopher Newport, to name but a few. These are the celebrated seafaring men who have gone down in British history as great explorers and defenders of the realm. In addition, there were high-ranking naval admirals and reformers such as Sir John Hawkins and his son Sir Richard Hawkins, who were both involved in the business, not to mention the many corrupt colonial governors, such as Sir Thomas Modyford, who supervised the whole operation from their luxurious plantation retreats in the West Indies, treading a precarious line between satisfying public opinion – which meant hanging the culprits – and issuing pardons so that the mayhem could continue.

## THE TREASURE FLEETS

Not surprisingly, given this encouragement by the state, piracy reached a level where world trade was being seriously undermined, with pirates thronging all the major shipping routes. Any kind of sea voyage was a hazardous business, and ships carrying precious cargo were forced to travel in convoy, armed to the teeth. The Spanish treasure fleet was a case in point. King Philip II of Spain had imposed such heavy taxes on his colonies in the Americas that galleons groaning with gold, silver, gems and spices, were constantly

sailing across the world, a tantalizing target for pirates everywhere. In the same way, the rich Mughal fleet became a focal point for all kinds of adventurers; and later, the British ships of the East India Company were similarly targeted. By the end of the 17th century, a well-established sailing route known as the Pirate Round had developed, leading from the western Atlantic, round Africa, past Madagascar, to India and beyond.

Eventually, the situation became completely untenable. Where once the pirates and privateers had aided the cause of British imperialism and economic expansion, they now threatened it. In addition, by the mid 18th century the British crown had wrested a great deal of territory from Spain in the Caribbean, and no longer had such a pressing need to maintain the privateers. As a result, the authorities clamped down on piracy, and little by little, it subsided. The 'golden age' had come to an end.

## MYTH OR FACT?

Yet this colourful period in history has continued to delight successive generations. Adventure stories about swashbuckling buccaneers, whether in books, films or video games, are still, in the 21st century, a perennial source of entertainment. Not surprisingly – since many of these are aimed at children – the violent and often rather squalid reality of the pirate life has been glossed over. But for the more serious student of history, the question remains – how much of what we know about pirates and privateers is myth, and how much fact?

The answer is that most of the features we attribute to pirates have some basis in reality, though they are often exaggerated. For example, we know that a few pirates did bury treasure: for example, the notorious pirate Captain Kidd left a cache of gold, silver, rubies, diamonds, candlesticks and porringers on Gardiner Island near New York (though before he returned to claim it, he was hanged). However, there are few other reports of such activity, so we must assume

that it was uncommon.

We also know that some pirates dressed in garish clothes: Calico Jack got his nickname from the gaily coloured calico clothing he wore, while Black Bart was described as going into battle 'dressed in a rich crimson damask waistcoat and breeches, a red feather in his hat, a gold chain round his neck, with a diamond cross hanging to it …'. But in reality, of course, most pirates would have been ragged and poorly dressed. In the same way, the image of the pirate with the eyepatch and the wooden leg also has some truth to it: pirates did get wounded in battle, and seldom received proper medical attention, so that they often ended up with serious disabilities. However, not all of them looked like Long John Silver.

And what of the Jolly Roger, the pirate flag with the skull and crossbones? Again, we know that several pirates, including Blackbeard, Stede Bonnet, Calico Jack and Thomas Tew, used this design in various forms, but in most cases it seems that the pirate ships flew a plain black flag.

Were there really women pirates? Yes, but they were few and far between. They include Mary Read, who dressed as a man, her friend Anne Bonney, and others such as Mary Crickett, Charlotte de Berry, Grace O'Malley, and, the most successful female pirate of all: Ching Shih, a former prostitute, who led a Chinese pirate fleet consisting of over 1,000. These were women who had escaped from lives of poverty, prostitution, servitude or arranged marriage, to live and work alongside the rough-and-ready pirate bands; they were courageous, charismatic individuals, but it must be remembered that, like the men, they were also for the most part violent, bloodthirsty criminals.

## PIRATE DEMOCRACY

Much of what we know about pirates comes from Alexander Exquemelin's *History of the Bouccaneers of America*, published in 1678. Exquemelin had been a barber-surgeon to the pirate Henry Morgan. Another source is Captain Johnson's *A General History of the Robberies and Murders of the Most Notorious Pyrates*, published in 1724. However, this is considered by most historians to be a somewhat sensationalized account.

The rather fanciful Captain Johnson reports that in the late 17th century, the pirate Thomas Tew set up a utopian colony on the island of Madagascar, where pirates, ex-slaves, and other outcasts from society lived a life of ease in harmony with nature and each other. This is almost certainly a fabrication, but there is evidence that pirate communities did actually operate in a fairly egalitarian way. The captain of a pirate ship and his second-in-command, the quartermaster, were usually democratically elected, and pirates shared the proceeds of their spoils according to their rank. They even operated a primitive social security system: for the loss of an arm, a pirate would receive 600 pieces of eight, for an eye, 100, and so on.

## PIRACY TODAY

Today, as in the past, piracy continues in areas of the world where poverty and political instability are the norm. Pirates operate mostly off the coast of Somalia, in the Straits of Malacca, in the South China Sea, and in the Niger Delta, using small ships, speedboats, guns and mobile phones. Some groups are linked with organized crime, while others are independent. Their favoured method is to take hostages and demand ransoms; in some instances, cash supplies on-board ship are targeted, along with personal belongings of the crews and passengers. Murder of hostages is thankfully rare, and most of the attacks at sea occur without fatalities, but piracy results in considerable damage to world shipping, currently estimated at over $13 billion per year. And in the first decade of the new millennium, as the world enters a recession and poverty becomes more widespread, piracy looks set to continue for the foreseeable future, reminding us that behind the romance of outlaw life on the ocean wave lies a rather more sordid reality – of greed, extortion and violence.

# Pirates

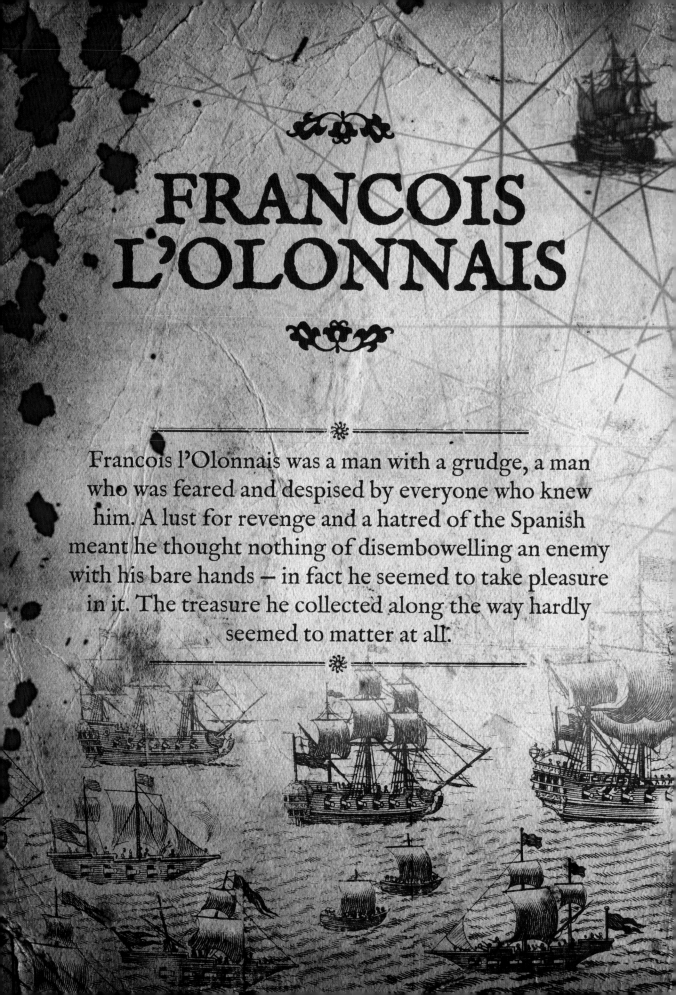

# FRANCOIS L'OLONNAIS

Francois l'Olonnais was a man with a grudge, a man who was feared and despised by everyone who knew him. A lust for revenge and a hatred of the Spanish meant he thought nothing of disembowelling an enemy with his bare hands — in fact he seemed to take pleasure in it. The treasure he collected along the way hardly seemed to matter at all.

The French pirate l'Olonnais has become notorious as one of the cruellest and most vicious pirates in history. During his lifetime he was feared and hated as a man who would think nothing of disembowelling a fellow human being with his bare hands, or torturing a victim in such a way that his eyes popped out of his head – literally. He had a particular animosity toward the Spanish, and not surprisingly, given his treatment of innocent citizens in the Spanish settlements he raided, the feeling was mutual.

### PLAYING DEAD

He was born Jean-David Nau in 1635, in a place called Sables d'Olonne in the Vendee, France. The name of his hometown later gave him his nickname, l'Olonnais – the man from Olonne. As a young man, he became an indentured servant and was taken to work in the Caribbean. When he had worked out the terms of his contract, he was set free and began to travel around the islands, eking out a living as best he could. Before long, he had teamed up with local buccaneers and was robbing ships plying the Spanish Maine. He soon developed a following, because he was a competent seaman and a successful pirate.

Early in his career, he and his crewmates were shipwrecked off the coast of Mexico. While they were in disarray, they were attacked by a group of Spanish soldiers, who killed nearly all of them. L'Olonnais only survived by covering himself in the blood of his companions and pretending he was dead. It may have been this experience that gave him his lifelong hatred of the Spanish, and his taste for revenge.

### MASS BEHEADING

After escaping with his life, l'Olonnais gathered together a motley band of thieves and took to robbing towns and settlements on land, one of the first pirates of his day to do so. In one instance, a Spanish rescue party was sent from Havana to protect the town's civilian population.

L'Olonnais beheaded all of them except one, sending him back to Havana with the message, 'I shall never henceforward give quarter to any Spaniard whatsoever.'

By now, l'Olonnais was a force to be reckoned with. In 1666, he set sail with a large fleet of pirate ships to ransack the city of Maracaibo in Venezuela. On the way, the pirates attacked a Spanish galleon loaded with gold coins, precious jewels and *cacao* (cocoa or raw chocolate). They then disembarked at Maracaibo and crept up on the city by land, rather than sailing into the harbour. In this way, they captured the heavily armed fort that protected the city. When they got there, they found that the citizens had hidden their treasures, but l'Olonnais was undeterred. He tortured them without mercy until they admitted where the booty was, and then he and his men made off with it.

### TEARING OUT A MAN'S HEART

Their next destination was the city of Gibraltar. Here, they managed to fight off a larger force, killing hundreds of soldiers but sustaining fewer than 100 casualties themselves. Having decimated the opposition, l'Olonnais and his men then toured the island, killing the inhabitants and stealing whatever they could find, be it slaves, silver, gold or precious gems. In accordance with the traditions of piracy, the booty was divided between each of his men.

Not surprisingly, l'Olonnais became a hero among the pirates of the region. Lured by the promise of untold riches, they flocked to his leadership. Soon he was leading a band of more than 500 freebooters on various raids against other Spanish cities in the region, including Puerto Cabello and San Pedro. When he met resistance from the Spanish soldiers guarding San Pedro, he terrified them by choosing one victim, cutting open his breast, pulling out his heart with his bare hands, and eating it. He went on to devise ever more cruel tortures, such as cutting into a victim piece-by-piece, progressing from slices of flesh to entire limbs. Another of his favourite tortures was to tie a string around a victim's eyes and tighten it so that the eyes jumped out of their sockets. This practice was known at the time as 'woolding'.

## JUST DESERTS

Eventually, after many more brutal attacks on innocent Spaniards, l'Olonnais met his match in the shape of the native inhabitants of Darien, Panama. When he landed there with his band of pirates, they captured him, and realizing that he was the legendary l'Olonnais, the man who had raped, pillaged and tortured his way through South America, they decided to wreak their own revenge on him. After tearing him into pieces while he was still alive, they tossed his limbs and torso into a great fire, reducing his body to ashes so that nothing of him remained. It was a fitting end to a life of barbarism, and few mourned his loss.

# HENRY MORGAN

---

As a young man Henry Morgan set out for the New World in search of a life of adventure, but his wildest dreams could not foretell what danger and excitement lay in store. He amassed considerable respectability, wealth and power thanks to some well-connected familial contacts and a bit of good old-fashioned hell-raising, before a kiss-and-tell exposé eventually revealed him for what he truly was — one of the most blood-thirsty pirates ever to have sailed the seven seas.

---

enry Morgan was one of the most successful pirates of the 17th century. For most of his career, he had the protection of the British government, who employed him as a privateer in their battle with the Spanish over colonial rule in the New World. Because of this privileged position, he was able to do more or less as he pleased, making raids on cities, towns and settlements, and amassing enormous personal wealth in the process. There were reports that these raids entailed savage violence and brutality, including the torture of ordinary citizens, but he was quick to refute these stories, in one case suing a publisher who dared to suggest his methods were anything but civilized.

Occasionally, he went too far, as in his storming of Panama, for which he was arrested; but eventually, because of the political considerations of the day, instead of being hung, he was knighted for his pains. He was one of the very few pirates in history to retire gracefully from his buccaneering days, living out his last days as the wealthy owner of a plantation in Jamaica, rather than being hung as a thief. To this day, there are those who continue to regard him as an illustrious defender of English colonial rule, rather than a violent, marauding thug.

## A Life of Adventure

Henry Morgan was born in 1635 in Llanrumney, Wales, which was then part of Monmouthshire, but is now an area of Cardiff. He was the eldest son of a well-to-do squire, Robert Morgan, but as a young man, he left home and travelled to the West Indies to seek his fortune.

He was lucky to find that, in the New World, there were numerous opportunities for a life of adventure. It was open season in the Caribbean for all manner of rogues and buccaneers, whether under the protection of the crown or independent. Moreover, Morgan had friends in high places, which was to help his career enormously.

In 1665, Jamaica was conquered by the British, and shortly afterwards, Henry's uncle Edward was installed as Lieutenant Governor of the new colony. To cement the relationship, Henry married Edward's daughter Mary, his cousin, and thus, through his family connections, gained access to the corridors of power among the colonial rulers of the region.

## Admiral Morgan

Morgan is thought to have begun his career in the naval fleet, under the command of one Christopher Myngs. He also made expeditions to Honduras and Mexico, where several towns and settlements were raided. He then sailed under the seasoned privateer Edward Mansfield, who was backed by Sir Thomas Modyford, the Governor of Jamaica. Modyford's expedition successfully took over the islands of Santa Catalina and Providence, after much resistance from the Spanish. However, some time later, Mansfield was captured and killed by the enemy. This proved to be Morgan's break, as he was chosen to take over command. Thus it was that Morgan became an admiral of the British fleet.

## The Triumph of Portobello

By now, Morgan had become an important figure in the British Navy. Accordingly, he was given greater responsibility and more resources were laid at his disposal. He was given the task of making a raid on the principal town of Haiti, with a fleet of 10 ships and 500 men. The sacking of the town was successfully accomplished, although many lost their lives in the fighting, and there were criticisms that the victors bagged too many of the spoils for themselves.

Morgan then set his sights on a far bigger prize: the town of Portobello, which is now in modern-day Panama. This proved to be his claim to fame. Not only did he ransack the town, he also managed to free a number of British prisoners who had been languishing there under harsh conditions. When news of his victory reached the British, he became a hero over night. The famous market street in London, Portobello Road, was named in his honour, to commemorate the freeing of the prisoners.

## COMMON PIRATES?

Naturally enough, these raids involved a great deal of bloodshed. Moreover, the plunderers were allowed to divide their spoils between them, with no regard for the property rights of those they attacked, and little respect for their superiors in the British government. However, the scandal of the marauding privateers, who behaved no better than common pirates, was hushed up by the Admiralty in Britain, who continued to trumpet Morgan as a hero. In addition, the Governor of Jamaica drew a veil over the violence of the raids, and even organized celebrations on the crew's return from battle. It seemed that, as long as Morgan did the authorities' bidding, they were prepared to turn a blind eye to the excesses of his attacks.

Before long, Morgan was sent off again to conduct raids on Spanish settlements in Cuba and Venezuela. He also destroyed three Spanish ships while at sea, provoking the wrath of the Spanish, who began to threaten attacks on Jamaica. The hostilities escalated, and soon Morgan was planning an attack on Panama, one of the wealthiest cities in the New World, with a force of over 1,000 men, even though this contravened a treaty made between England and Spain.

## SUED FOR LIBEL

In the event, the sacking of Panama was not quite as successful as Morgan had envisaged. Most of the city's valuables had been loaded onto a ship and guarded closely, so that the freebooters could not get at it. Morgan and his men did as much damage as they could, but they emerged with a great deal less plunder than they had hoped. The inhabitants told tales of torture and arson, and this time, in an effort to placate the Spanish, with whom Britain had just signed a treaty, Morgan was arrested and hauled up before the British authorities. However, when relations between the Spanish and the British subsequently deteriorated, the charges were dropped, and

instead of being charged with murder, Morgan was knighted. He was also promoted to Lieutenant Governor of Jamaica, and retired there to live a life of ease on a large plantation.

## THE TIDE TURNS

Morgan's reputation then took a turn for the worse with the publication of a book by a former confidante, a barber-surgeon named Alexander Exquemelin, which detailed his bloodthirsty exploits. Morgan immediately mounted a libel suit and successfully secured damages of £200 against the publisher, together with a promise to retract the accusations. However, the book did nothing to enhance Morgan's standing, and from then on he became infamous as one of the most bloodthirsty pirates in history.

## FINAL YEARS

Although Morgan was by now a very rich and powerful man, the life of a grandee did not seem to suit him. He grew bored, and began to drink heavily, offending polite society with his rowdy behaviour. Little by little, his social standing deteriorated. He became overweight and his health suffered. Eventually he fell seriously ill, and was described by his medical advisor, Sir Hans Sloane, as being 'yellow and swollen'. It seems likely that he was suffering from liver failure as a result of his heavy drinking. Sloane reported that Henry Morgan died in his bed on 25 August 1688.

RIGHT: This engraving shows Henry Morgan and his pirates mistreating the citizens of Maracaibo on the Spanish Main, in 1669.

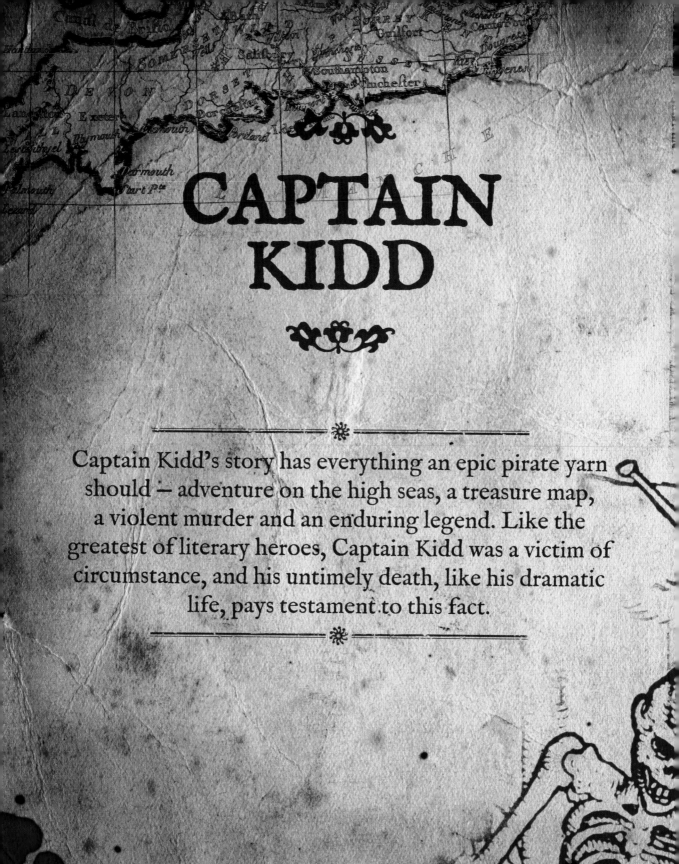

# CAPTAIN KIDD

Captain Kidd's story has everything an epic pirate yarn should — adventure on the high seas, a treasure map, a violent murder and an enduring legend. Like the greatest of literary heroes, Captain Kidd was a victim of circumstance, and his untimely death, like his dramatic life, pays testament to this fact.

aptain Kidd will forever be remembered as the pirate who left a cache of hidden treasure on an island, hoping one day to return and reclaim it. In the event, he was unable to get back to the island, because he was hung in England for piracy, but the legend of the buried treasure, and the map, lived on, becoming a central part of pirate lore.

## SUCCESSFUL PRIVATEER

William Kidd was born around 1645 in Scotland. Accounts vary as to his place of birth. Recent research suggests that it was Dundee, but according to the Newgate Calendar, which recorded the misdeeds of criminals at the time, he came from Greenock. When he was five years old, his father died, and his family moved to New York, then a colony of Britain. As an adult, he became a sailor, working in the service of several prominent colonial governors.

He soon rose to the rank of captain, and was commissioned to attack French vessels during England's war with France, a task he accomplished with such élan that he became well known among the London traders. He travelled to England to seek privateering work, and while he was there, received a commission from the Governor of New York, The Earl of Bellomont, to command a new ship, the *Adventure Galley*. This was a state-of-the-art warship armed with 34 cannons and a crew of 80 men. Kidd's brief was to attack all French shipping on the high seas, and he was also asked, as a side earner, to attack pirate ships as well. At first he refused, knowing the severity of the penalties for lawlessness on the high seas, but under pressure from the investors, he eventually agreed.

## ILL-FATED VOYAGE

The project seemed ill-fated from the start. As the ship made its way down the Thames, it was ordered to lower its flags in deference to Royal Navy shipping, but instead, Kidd's sailors took down their trousers and waggled their bottoms in the air. For this silly misdemeanour, the ship was boarded and many of the crew taken off. Thus, when he reached New York, Kidd had to hastily assemble more sailors. The new recruits were, for the most part, a rough and ready lot, many of them former pirates.

The ship set sail for Madagascar, but the problems continued. There was an outbreak of cholera on-board ship, and many died. To make matters worse, the supposedly modern ship began to spring leaks everywhere. Weakened and demoralized, the crew began to demand that Kidd turn pirate.

## MURDER OR MANSLAUGHTER?

Afraid of mutiny, Kidd engaged in a fight with the ship's gunner, William Moore, who was pressing him to attack a passing Dutch ship. Kidd called Moore a lousy dog, to which Moore responded that if he was, it was Kidd's fault. At this, Kidd smashed him over the head with a bucket, killing him dead.

Although it was common at the time for captains to discipline men harshly, murder was unusual, and could be punished by hanging. Kidd, however, believed that he would not be executed for such a crime, having friends in high places at home.

RIGHT: An illustration depicting the moment of William Moore's murder at the hands of Captain Kidd.

## TURNING PIRATE

As the voyage progressed, Kidd decided that the only viable option open to him was to become a pirate. After this, his fortunes improved. His most successful venture was the capture of the *Quedagh Merchant*, an Armenian ship loaded with treasure. When it transpired that it was captained by an Englishman, Kidd reportedly asked his crew to return it, but the crew refused, so in the end Kidd gave in, making sure to keep the passes in the captain's possession, so that he could show them as evidence if he was later tried for piracy.

## BURYING THE TREASURE

Eventually, after many more adventures at sea, Kidd decided to return home to New York to clear his name. On the way, he stopped off at Gardiner's Island near New York, to bury some treasure for his retirement. The treasure consisted of gold, silver, rubies, diamond, candlesticks and porringers. Kidd gave the proprietors of the island, Mr and Mrs Gardiner, a piece of gold cloth and a bag of sugar in exchange for their help, and warned them that if the treasure was touched before he got back, they would be killed.

Kidd then returned home, hoping that if he turned himself in, he would receive clemency from the authorities as a result of his connections. However, once he did so, his powerful friends deserted him. He was imprisoned and put into solitary confinement, suffering very harsh conditions there. He was then sent to England for questioning.

## HIDEOUS DEATH

In England, Kidd found himself a political pawn. There was a new Tory government in office, who were hoping to discredit their opponents, the Whigs, by getting Kidd to name the officials who had backed him. But Kidd refused, thinking that they would help him in his hour of need. He was wrong.

He was imprisoned at Newgate and charged with the murder of William Moore and five counts of piracy. The passes he had obtained from the *Quedagh Merchant* were not shown as evidence, and he received no legal representation. On 23 May 1701 he was hanged at Execution Dock in Wapping. During the hanging, the rope broke. Kidd was left gasping for air while another rope was found, and the hanging performed for a second time. When Kidd was finally dead, his body was put in an iron cage and hung up over the Thames as a warning to other pirates of the fate that would befall them.

## SUNKEN GALLEON

As for the treasure on Gardiner's Island, it was dug up and used as evidence against Kidd in his trial – unfairly, since some of the treasure had been bought, not plundered, and there were papers to prove it. Many continue to believe that Kidd also buried treasure on other islands around the world, pointing to the existence of a map among Kidd's possessions showing the China Sea, a lagoon, a smuggler's cove and some treacherous reefs, but to date no buried treasure has been found.

There was however, an exciting discovery in 2007, when a scuba diver came across an underwater shipwreck off the coast of Catalina Island in the Caribbean. A team of archaeologists and anthropologists confirmed that this was almost certainly the wreckage of the *Quedagh Merchant*, verifying that the size of the cannons tallied exactly with the historical records. The team was thrilled with the discovery, describing the legendary sunken galleon as 'a living museum'.

## TRAGIC STORY

Today, it seems likely that Captain Kidd was unfairly hanged. He probably killed gunner Moore by accident, and although he undoubtedly indulged in occasional piracy, along with many privateers of the time, most of his voyages appear to have been perfectly legal. Until the age of 50, when he took on the ill-fated task of commanding the *Adventure Galley*, he was clearly a respected man with the support and friendship of high-ranking figures such as Benjamin Fletcher, Governor of New York. But when he ran into trouble, they deserted him, and he was strung up like a common thief, earning the reputation he carries today.

LEFT: Captain Kidd and his crew bury their treasure on Gardiner's Island.

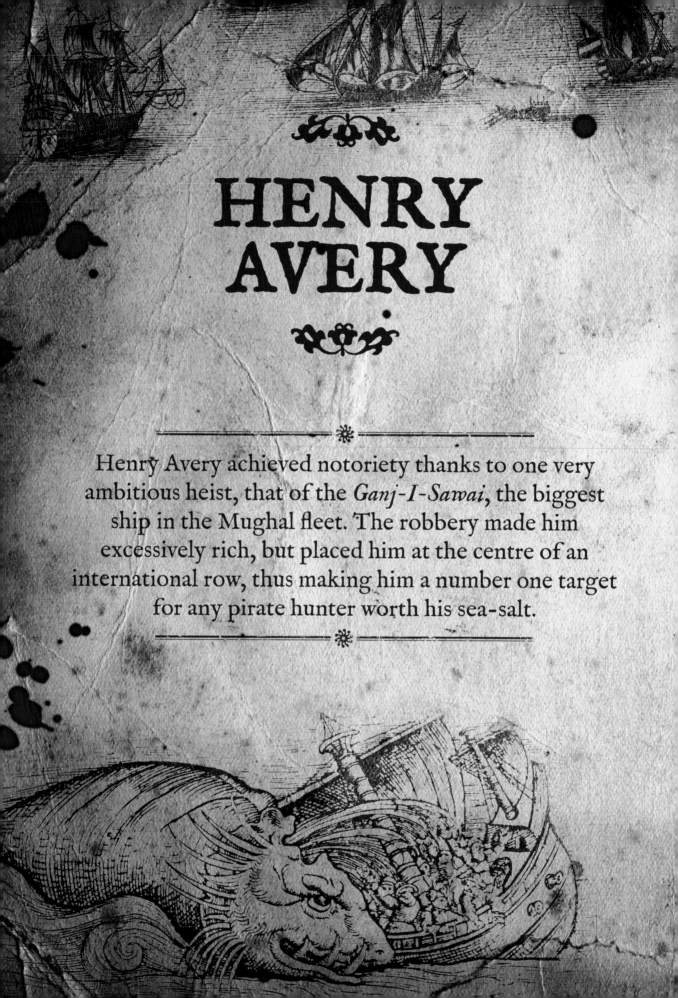

# HENRY AVERY

Henry Avery achieved notoriety thanks to one very ambitious heist, that of the *Ganj-I-Sawai*, the biggest ship in the Mughal fleet. The robbery made him excessively rich, but placed him at the centre of an international row, thus making him a number one target for any pirate hunter worth his sea-salt.

enry Avery, or Every – his actual name is the subject of some controversy – has gone down in history as the 'arch pirate' who made a fortune from a double hit on two ships in 1694. The ships he attacked were prize vessels of the Islamic Mughal empire, which at the time ruled most of the Indian subcontinent. They were travelling to India via the Mandab Strait, a narrow passage connecting the Red Sea to the Gulf of Aden, loaded with gold, silver, diamonds and other treasure.

Avery and his men overwhelmed both ships and, after fierce fighting, made off with their entire contents. The loss of such a great fortune – worth millions, even in today's terms – created a huge furore, and seriously damaged trade relations between the Mughals and the British East India Company. Avery became a wanted man, exempt from the pardons and acts of grace often given to privateers and pirates, and with a price on his head. In fact, he became a target for other bounty-hunting pirates, including the notorious Captain Kidd, who were given incentives by the government to catch him. However, Avery managed to elude capture – although some say he spent his last years in poverty – and became one of the few pirates to die of natural causes.

## A SALTY SEA DOG

Avery is thought to have been born in the seafaring town of Plymouth, and to have spent his early adulthood at sea on merchant ships. According to various sources, he was a sailor in the Royal Navy for a time, taking part in the bombardment of a pirate base in Algiers in 1671. Other reports suggest that he was the captain of a freighter carrying logs, and that he also spent some time as a pirate in the Caribbean Sea. He then moved into the slave trade, buying slaves off the West African coast. Rumour had it that once he had bought the slaves, he would seize the traders as well, and chain them up on the ships

too. He also used a variety of pseudonyms to escape detection, often calling himself Benjamin Bridgeman, Long Ben, or John Avery. Clearly, he was a man to whom the notion of fair dealing meant absolutely nothing at all.

But for what happened next, Avery might have remained a footnote to history, just one of many disreputable buccaneers earning a living in any way they could on the lawless high seas. However, as it turned out he succeeded in becoming one of the most notorious pirates of all time, on the basis of one single expedition that netted him a fortune beyond his wildest dreams.

## TREASURE SHIP

In 1694, Avery was working for a Captain Gibson aboard a large privateer ship, the *Charles II*. The captain was well known to be a drunk, and the crew were becoming restless because he did not pay them regularly. Avery planned a successful mutiny, dumped Gibson on shore, and took over command of the ship, renaming it the *Fancy*. He then set off for the Cape of Good Hope, and once at the Cape Verde islands, managed to take three English merchant ships. Next, he put into port, and had his ship redesigned so that it sailed faster. He subsequently took a French pirate ship, recruiting more men to his crew, and sailed on to the Mandab Strait, where he was lucky enough to encounter the biggest ship in the Mughal fleet, the *Ganj-I-Sawai*.

First, Avery attacked the ship's companion vessel, the *Fateh Muhammed*, overwhelming the crew and making off with the goods on-board. Then he caught up with the *Ganj-I-Sawai* and opened fire. A fierce battle ensued, and even though the ship was bigger and better armed than the *Fancy*, Avery won the day. A large part of the victory was due to luck. At one stage, one of the larger ship's cannons exploded, disorienting the crew and killing several. In addition, the Mughal ship's captain was said to have turned tail and rushed below decks to hide with his concubines, leaving his crew to fight on without him.

## Rape and Pillage

Once the fighting was over, Avery and his men behaved with the utmost cruelty, inflicting rape, murder and brutality on the hapless crew and passengers of the ship, who numbered several hundred. Muslim women were reported to have killed themselves to avoid rape at the hands of their captors. Avery then ransacked the ship, taking gold, silver and gems worth millions, and then abandoned it, leaving the survivors to drift at sea. The pirates divided the spoils between them and set off once more, taking some of the Muslim women with them as concubines.

The next problem – and it was one that beset Avery until his dying day – was how to sell the booty. When news came out of the robbery, the British government put a price on Avery's head,

so that he was unable to buy a pardon or take refuge anywhere, even in the most lawless parts of the West Indies. Because of this, the pirate band split up, each going their own way to avoid capture and retribution.

## Mysterious Disappearance

According to one account, Avery then travelled back to England, via Ireland, and took up residence in the small Devonian town of Bideford. Ironically, his diamonds were so valuable that he could not sell them on the open market, for fear of being discovered, so he offloaded them onto some merchant 'friends' – who then blackmailed him, so that he was forced to live out his days on the breadline. Alternative reports suggest that he retired to a remote spot in the West Indies and spent his old age as he'd intended, surrounded by luxury. But whatever the case, there are no records concerning him after 1696, so we will never know the truth. We do know, however, that he managed to escape the fate of many pirates – being strung up on the hangman's gibbet as a warning to all.

# THOMAS TEW

Thomas Tew was something of a visionary in pirate terms. He is best known for pioneering the famous Pirate Round, and for founding Libertalia, a legendary pirate haven and experimental community which is said to have existed in a remote part of Madagascar. The source of many a swashbuckling pirate tale, Tew's death was not so romantic — he was blown to smithereens during an attack on a Mughal convoy, when he caught a cannonball in the gut.

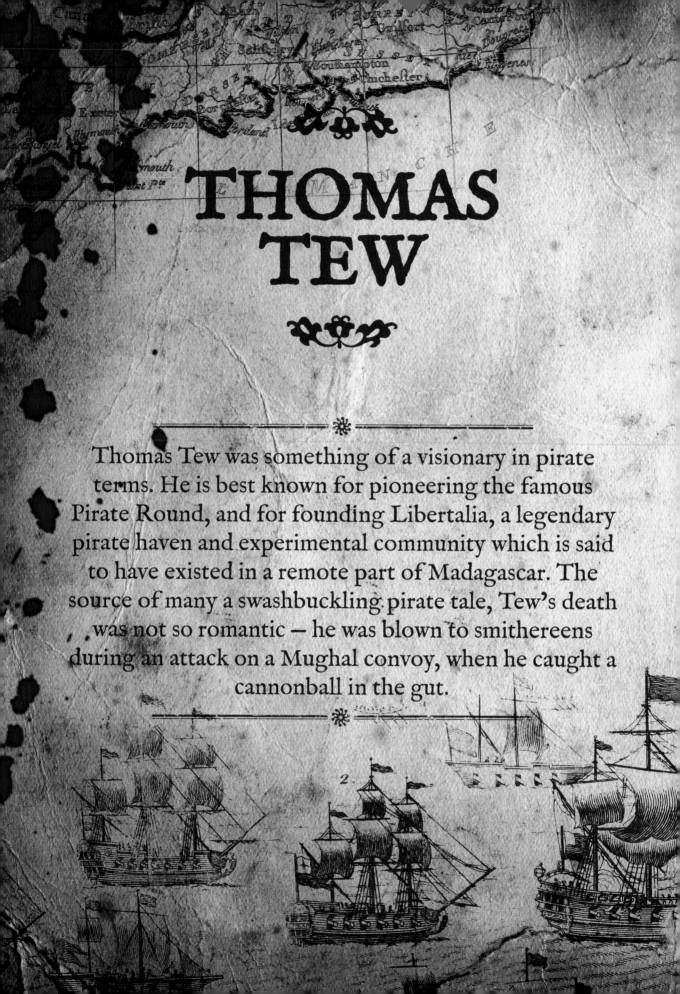

homas Tew was a 17th century pirate who for many years enjoyed the high life in New York with his wife and daughters. However, he finally met a sorry end while engaged in an attack on a Mughal convoy in the Red Sea, being blown apart by a cannon. Today, he is best remembered as one of the pioneers of the Pirate Round, a route followed by pirates that targeted trade ships sailing from the western Atlantic, around Africa to Madagascar, and then on to Yemen and India. Many of the ships that plied these waters were owned by the East India Company, and promised rich pickings. Tew was also said to be one of the founders of the legendary pirate enclave Libertalia, an anarchist community set up in a remote part of Madagascar. Whether or not Libertalia actually existed continues to be the subject of some debate.

## PRIVATEER TURNED PIRATE

Very little is known about the early life of Thomas Tew, but it is thought that he was born in Maidford, Northamptonshire. Although he later claimed to have a long line of ancestry in Rhode Island, it is likely that he arrived there as a young child when his family emigrated there. He grew up in Newport and as a young man, took up a seafaring career, returning to his hometown as often as he could. He married and had two daughters, and by all accounts enjoyed the comforts of domestic life, although he was often away at sea.

The exact nature of his sailing expeditions was never made clear to his family and friends at home, but most took it that he was engaged as a privateer, hired by the authorities to attack French and Spanish ships as part of the British offensive in the colonial wars. However, at some point in his career, he abandoned the semi-legal practise of privateering and became a pirate, attacking ships at random for his own profit, along with a band of bloodthirsty ruffians. But as long as he kept bringing in the money, on his visits home he and his family remained part of an elite New York social scene, and not too many questions were asked.

## STRIKING LUCKY

In 1692, Tew was backed by the governor of Bermuda, and given an armed ship, the *Amity*, with a crew of over 40 men. His mission was to fight the French in Africa, but once out of port, he decided to head for the Red Sea instead, to hunt down one of the Indian ships that often crossed there. He soon struck lucky, attacking a huge ship loaded with gold, silver, spices, silk and precious jewels. Unusually, there were no casualties, as the ship's crew offered no resistance, despite being heavily armed.

Amazed at their good fortune, Tew and his men stopped off in Madagascar to share out the spoils and then sailed back to Newport. By now, he was an extremely rich man, with a fortune of over £5,000, a vast amount of money in those days. Friends flocked to him, including the governor of New York, Benjamin Fletcher, who soon backed him on another voyage.

## BLOWN TO SMITHEREENS

This time, Tew was not so lucky. When he went back to his hunting ground, he found that it was swarming with other pirates, hoping to strike lucky as he had. One of them was Henry Avery

in his speedy, heavily armed ship the *Fancy*. Tew decided to join forces with Avery, and along with a number of other pirates, helped attack a Mughal convoy in the Mandab Strait. While attacking one of the ships, the *Fateh Muhammed*, Tew was struck down, shot by a cannon in the stomach. His crew immediately surrendered and were captured, but were later set free when Avery arrived and overwhelmed the Indian ship. Ironically, the strike on the *Fateh Muhammed* and its sister ship, the *Ganj-I-Sawai* yielded untold treasure and made Avery famous, but Tew was not alive to enjoy his share of the booty.

## PIRATE UTOPIA

After his death, the legend of Thomas Tew lived on, both as the inventor of the Pirate Round, the passage around Africa to India, and as the founder of a pirate commune, Libertalia. (The account of Libertalia comes from one source – that of Captain Johnson's *A General History of the Pyrates*, published in 1724 and thought by many to be the work of Daniel Defoe.) He was also alleged, while in Madagascar, to have had an affair with a Malagasy queen and fathered a boy named Ratsimilaho, who later grew up to rule a large region of the island. Whether or not this story is true remains unclear, but the idea of a romance between a swashbuckling pirate and an exotic island queen is undoubtedly one that continues to fascinate.

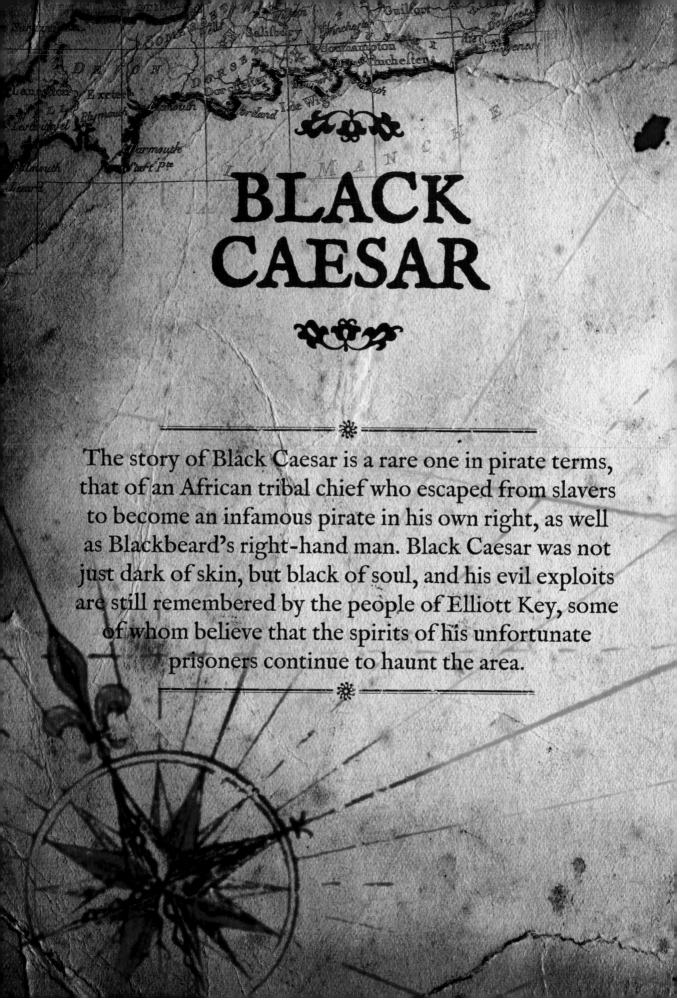

# BLACK CAESAR

The story of Black Caesar is a rare one in pirate terms, that of an African tribal chief who escaped from slavers to become an infamous pirate in his own right, as well as Blackbeard's right-hand man. Black Caesar was not just dark of skin, but black of soul, and his evil exploits are still remembered by the people of Elliott Key, some of whom believe that the spirits of his unfortunate prisoners continue to haunt the area.

Fig. 1

There are many pirates who were dubbed 'black' – Bartholomew Roberts for instance, nicknamed Black Bart – but in most instances this referred to the state of their souls rather than the colour of their skin. The case of Black Caesar was different. He really was a black man, an African slave turned pirate, who plied his trade around the Florida Keys for almost 10 years before being caught and hanged.

## AFRICAN CHIEF

Legend has it that Black Caesar was originally the chief of an African tribe. He was often hunted by slavers, but owing to his keen intelligence and physical prowess, he usually outwitted his pursuers. However, in one instance, he was tricked into going aboard a merchant ship, along with 20 of his men. The captain of the ship, a slave trader, showed the Africans a watch, and promised there were more precious goods on-board for them to see. They were curious, and followed him on-board. To begin with, all went well, and the captain entertained the men royally, with feasting and music. But unbeknown to them, the crew were raising anchor as they caroused, and before they knew it, they found themselves out at sea.

At first, Black Caesar and his tribesmen tried to escape, attacking the captain and his crew, but their captors were well armed with guns and pistols, and eventually they surrendered. They were trapped, and had to accept that they were now prisoners aboard a ship whose captain would undoubtedly sell them as slaves when it reached land. Angry at having been duped, Caesar refused to accept food or drink from any but one sailor in the crew who befriended him.

However, as luck would have it, Caesar did not have to wait long before a chance came to make his escape. The ship ran into a fierce hurricane, which proved a blessing in disguise. As the winds battered the ship, Black Caesar and his friend the sailor managed to row to shore on a longboat, where they waited out the storm together.

## OUTLAW COLONY

Stranded on shore, at a spot now called Elliott Key, the pair soon hit on a means of survival. When they saw a passing ship, they would row out in the lifeboat. Those aboard would let them onto the ship, thinking they were shipwrecked sailors. However, once on deck they would brandish their pistols, demand food and supplies of ammunition, and then row off again. As time went on, they would demand cargo as well, including gold, silver and precious gems. In one case, they brought back a woman as part of the booty. This proved a source of dispute, however, which ended when Black Caesar killed his former friend and claimed the woman for his own.

Much of what happened next appears to be conjecture, but legend has it that Black Caesar remained on a remote part of the Florida Keys, building up a sizeable community of pirates who subsisted by preying on passing ships. Despite the efforts of the authorities to catch them, they were able to escape, since they knew the terrain much better than their opponents did. Whenever a posse was sent out to hunt down Black Caesar and his pirates, they hid in various creeks and inlets (one of the creeks is now called Caesar's Creek), also camouflaging their boats and equipment. It was rumoured that as well as his ever-increasing band of pirates, Black Caesar also kept a large group of women, numbering over 100, who were used as concubines for the men. In addition, he was said to keep a supply of

prisoners from the ships, including children, so that he could blackmail their relations and gain ransoms for them. According to some reports, the prisoners were kept in terrible conditions, often starving to death when the pirates left them to make raids on passing ships. There were stories of children escaping and surviving by eating berries and shellfish, forming their own communities in the wild and growing up speaking strange languages that they had devised themselves. Even today, some inhabitants of Elliott Key believe that the area is haunted by the ghosts of these children.

## GUNPOWDER TRAIL

At some time during the turn of the 18th century, Black Caesar tired of life as a landlubber joined forces with the notorious pirate Blackbeard on-board the *Queen Anne's Revenge*. Together, this formidable pair attacked shipping in the Atlantic until a naval posse finally engaged them in battle on Ocracoke Island. Cornered, Black Caesar laid down a trail of gunpowder leading to some explosives, which he hoped would blow up his enemies. However, he was overpowered just before he ignited it. He was arrested and taken to Williamsburg, Virginia, where he was imprisoned. He was then put on trial, sentenced to death and hanged.

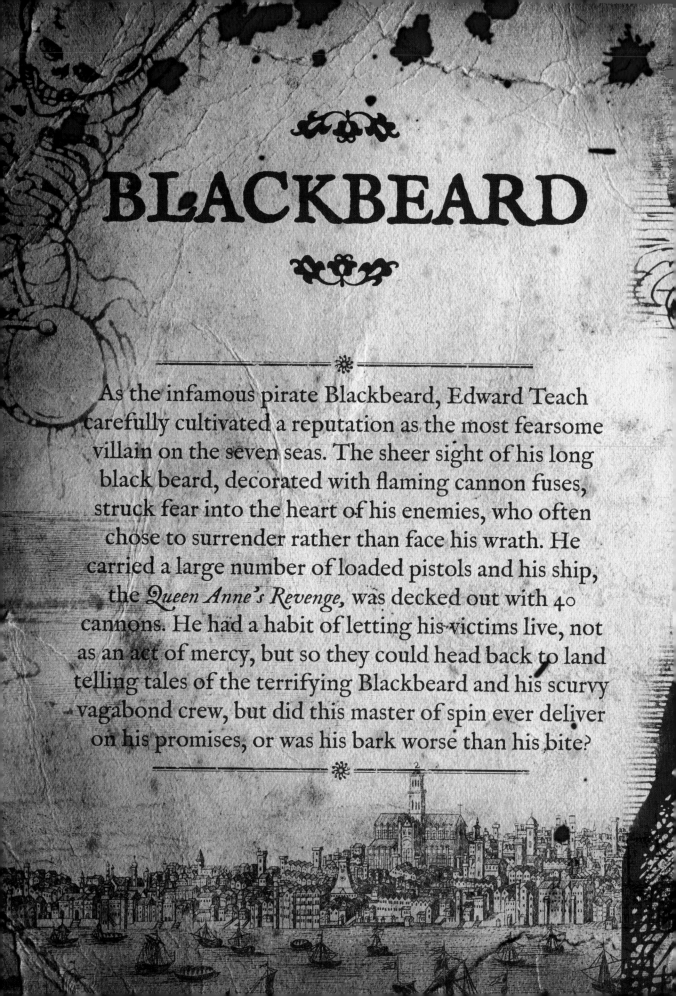

# BLACKBEARD

As the infamous pirate Blackbeard, Edward Teach carefully cultivated a reputation as the most fearsome villain on the seven seas. The sheer sight of his long black beard, decorated with flaming cannon fuses, struck fear into the heart of his enemies, who often chose to surrender rather than face his wrath. He carried a large number of loaded pistols and his ship, the *Queen Anne's Revenge*, was decked out with 40 cannons. He had a habit of letting his victims live, not as an act of mercy, but so they could head back to land telling tales of the terrifying Blackbeard and his scurvy vagabond crew, but did this master of spin ever deliver on his promises, or was his bark worse than his bite?

The notorious Blackbeard is perhaps the most famous pirate of all time. His reign of terror on the high seas took place in the early years of the 18th century. During that time, he became known for his terrifying appearance: when he attacked a ship, he plaited his beard with black ribbons, stuffed burning coils of ropes under his hat and decked himself with pistols, swords and knives, so that people fled from him in terror. However, it is thought that in fact he may never have killed anyone, relying on his appearance alone to terrorize his victims into submission. Whatever the case, there is no doubt that he was a cruel and lawless man, amassing vast riches and double-crossing his crew mates so that he could keep his ill-gotten gains for himself. He eventually came to a violent end in a bloody battle against Lieutenant Robert Maynard of the Royal Navy, at the instigation of the Governor of Virginia.

## REIGN OF TERROR

Blackbeard's real name was Edward Teach, or possibly Edward Thatch, and he is thought to have been born in Bristol, England. He went to sea at a young age, working on a British privateer ship in the West Indies during the War of Spanish Secession. Although the ship flew Queen Anne of Britain's flag, it was privately owned, and was at liberty not only to attack French and Spanish ships at random, but to keep any stolen booty as a reward. Not surprisingly, by the time the war ended, Teach and his crew mates had become expert sea robbers, operating independently outside the rule of law.

It was not long before the enterprising Teach acquired a stolen ship, named it *Queen Anne's Revenge*, equipped it with 40 guns, and assembled a large pirate crew. He began to attack merchant ships, many of which carried wealthy passengers. The pirates would sail near to a ship, hoist the flag of the ship's country, and so trick the captain into thinking that they were friends; then, as they drew near, they would hoist the pirate flag and let off a warning blast from the cannon. If the ship's captain did not immediately surrender – and he often did when he saw Blackbeard's flag – the pirates would move in.

Their first target would be the helmsman at the ship's wheel. As the ship rocked about in the water, the pirates would throw over their grappling hooks and swarm on to the deck, taking the crew and passengers hostage. Then they would ransack the ship, seizing everything of value – cargo such as grain, molasses and kegs of

An illustration showing Captain Maynard's sloop striking Blackbeard's ship the *Adventurer*.

rum, ammunition, rope and tools, liquor and food; and personal belongings from the passengers, such as gold coins and jewellery. Sometimes, not content with stealing everything on the ship, they would steal the ship as well! The lion's share of the spoils would always go to Blackbeard himself, of course.

## THE CHARLESTON BLOCKADE

In May 1718, Blackbeard sailed into Charleston, South Carolina, and waylaid all the cargo ships entering or leaving the port. One of them was filled with wealthy passengers, whom he took prisoner, locking them all up in the hold of the ship, and demanding a ransom for their release in the form of a medicine chest. His envoys were sent ashore, but instead of delivering their message, they went out carousing. Meanwhile, the pirates prepared the victims, including children, for hanging. At the last minute, the chest was delivered and the hostages were released.

Amazingly, the authorities of the day turned a blind eye to Blackbeard's escapades, and he was allowed to live in peace on a string of islands known as the Outer Banks in North Carolina, from where he preyed on passing ships travelling along the coastline. This was because he constantly bribed officials and supplied the local townspeople with cut-price stolen goods, including cloth and sugar. Eventually, Teach was given a royal pardon for his efforts, and retired to a favourite spot, Ocracoke Island. But the story was far from over.

## BLOODY BATTLE

Legend has it that Blackbeard gave a huge party on the island, inviting several other famous pirates and their crews to join him. The party went on for days. Bonfires were lit and there was much drinking, dancing and making merry. However, when news of the gathering reached the governor of Virginia, Alexander Spotswood, he decided that he had had enough of Blackbeard's antics, and sent Lieutenant Robert Maynard of the Royal Navy to deal with him.

On 11 November 1718 Maynard arrived with two small ships, the *Ranger* and *Jane*. There were a number of sandbars between the ships and the island where the pirates were carousing, so Maynard decided to wait until the tide came in before he attacked.

The pirates were outnumbered, but Blackbeard had the advantage of knowing the island's terrain well. Even though half his crew were drunk, he managed to steer his ship, the *Adventurer*, through a narrow sandbar. When the navy followed, their ships got stuck. They eventually freed themselves, but by then the pirates had the advantage and mounted a fierce attack, killing and wounding many of Maynard's men. Maynard persisted, however, until the *Adventurer* ran aground. Maynard brought his ship up alongside it, ordering his crew to hide below decks. The pirates thought the crew had all been killed and so boarded the ship. It was then that the naval crew rushed out with pistols, knives and swords, and a bloody battle began.

Accounts differ as to what happened next, but it is thought that during the battle, Maynard shot Blackbeard, while Blackbeard wounded Maynard with a cutlass. By the end of the battle, Blackbeard was reported to have been shot five times and stabbed over 20. Maynard then cut off Blackbeard's head, hung it from the bow of the ship, and took it back to the Governor, who awarded him a prize of £100, and ordered the head to be placed on a pole by the Hampton River. Today, the spot is known as Teach's Point.

# CHARLES VANE

Charles Vane's tale is a moral one. He was renowned, even in pirate terms, as a cruel and sadistic man who mistreated his crew and killed prisoners whenever he was given the opportunity. His inability to make friends and influence people ultimately meant he himself met a sticky end, on 22 March 1720, he was hung in chains as a warning to other pirates of the punishment that lay in wait.

The pirate Charles Vane was notorious not only as a menace to law and order on the high seas, but also among his fellow pirates as a cruel, selfish man. In particular, he was known for ignoring the pirate code which stipulated, albeit informally, that all booty should be shared among the crew. He was also disliked for his habit of torturing and murdering prisoners whenever he had the opportunity. In fact, he showed so little respect for his fellow human being, friend or foe, that when he finally came to need help, he found none, and met a sorry end as a result.

## TORTURE AND MURDER

We know from official records that Vane was born in 1680 in England, but there is no mention of where he grew up, or how he came to take up a career as a seafarer. However, he made his first appearance into the annals of criminal history in 1716, when he joined the crew of pirate Henry Jennings. Jennings' speciality was to prey on the ships and encampments of those who came to salvage sunken Spanish galleons, mostly off the coast of Florida. These ships were part of a treasure fleet that had sunk in 1715. Vane showed great skill at intimidating, attacking and robbing the salvagers, and soon progressed to captaincy of his own ship, sailing to the West Indies. In the Caribbean, he attacked a number of vessels and tortured the prisoners that he took. Pirates were not generally known for their genteel behaviour, but even so, it was unusual for a captain to inflict such unnecessary cruelty on those who had surrendered. Word of his bloodthirsty reputation spread, and on two occasions he was reported to the authorities for torturing the crew of two vessels that he had taken.

In a practise that proved disastrous for maintaining law and order on the high seas, notorious pirates were often given pardons by the authorities so that they could be enlisted as privateers. This meant that, instead of the pirates attacking ships at random for their own gain, they would be hired to attack enemy ships in the battle between the European powers – mainly English, French and Spanish – for control of the colonies. To this end, the Governor of the Bahamas, Woodes Rogers, visited the pirate haven of New Providence to offer pardons to the pirates there. Most of them enthusiastically accepted – after all, this was a chance to get off scot free, whatever heinous crimes they had committed, and, moreover, to gain new employment as privateers. Vane, however, was alone in rejecting Rogers' offer. As Rogers' warships approached, he set fire to a captured French ship he had in his possession, took a few pot shots at the naval warships and sailed off in the other direction.

## MUTINY AND REVENGE

Furious at his behaviour, Rogers had Vane pursued by a former pirate now working in his employ, one Benjamin Hornigold. However, Vane managed to give Hornigold the slip, and escaped to the Carolinas. Here, Vane continued to attack shipping, on one occasion mounting a blockade of Charleston Port, as the notorious pirate Blackbeard had done before him. One of Vane's conquests was a large ship carrying around 100 slaves.

The attacks on Charleston, not only by Vane but by other pirates operating in the area, infuriated the local population, forcing the Governor of South Carolina to act. He sent two

armed ships to track Vane down, commanded by Colonel William Rhett. Meanwhile, Vane was under attack from his own crew: his right-hand man, a pirate named Yeats, had gathered a posse of mutinous sailors under his command and sailed off at night in one of Vane's ships, taking with him a good deal of booty as well as the entire company of recently captured slaves. When Vane found out, he vowed to take his revenge, but for the moment there was nothing he could do.

## DRUNKEN REVELRY

Despite these problems, Vane managed to escape Rhett, and once again emerged unscathed from the Governor's offensive, eventually landing up in Ocracoke Island, North Carolina. Here, Vane met up with the notorious Blackbeard, and the two pirates, along with their men, embarked on a week of drunken revelry. When Vane sailed off again and began to plunder more ships, he found that Rhett was still after him. However, he was clever enough to outwit his opponents once more. He told his crew to talk about their plans to sail southwards in front of the sailors from the plundered ships. When Rhett caught up with the sailors, they gave him the information they'd overheard, so he set off southwards in hot pursuit of the pirates. Vane, however, had sailed north.

After a few months, Vane and his crew fell on hard times, since they had made few successful attacks. His crew, who showed very little loyalty towards him because of his cruelty, were beginning to grow restless. When they encountered a French ship, they urged their captain to attack it, which he did, exchanging a few rounds of gunfire; but on discovering it was a heavily armed warship, he felt it best to retreat. His crew disagreed, calling him a coward, and voting to make his quartermaster, Calico Jack Rackham, their new captain. Vane was unceremoniously ditched, and left only with a small ship and a few supporters to his name.

## HUNG UP IN CHAINS

Undeterred, Vane sailed to an area off the coast of Cuba, and began again from scratch, attacking small vessels and eking out a living. But further disaster was at hand. In February 1719, Vane and his crew encountered a hurricane while sailing through the Bay of Honduras, and were shipwrecked. Most of the men drowned during the storm, but Vane, along with one other pirate, managed to swim to an uninhabited island. There, they survived for months on fish and turtle meat, until a ship came by.

The ship was captained by one Captain Holford, a former 'friend' of Vane's. Unfortunately, Holford's previous experience of Vane's wily ways prompted him to give his old mate a wide berth, and he sailed straight past. Vane was eventually taken in by another passing ship, only to find Holford sailing up alongside and telling the rescuers that they had a dangerous pirate aboard. Vane was promptly arrested and imprisoned at Port Royal, Jamaica.

Despite the fact that Vane was evidently a deeply unpleasant man, who took a particular pleasure in torturing and murdering prisoners, he seems to have been somewhat more skilful and intelligent than most of the pirates of his day, remaining in open defiance of the authorities throughout his career, and outwitting them on many occasions. His downfall was that he treated his own men, and other sailors that he encountered along the way, just as badly as he treated everyone else: so that when at last he was shipwrecked and needed their help, he had no one to turn to.

After a swift trial, Charles Vane was hung on 22 March 1720. There were few who mourned his passing. Afterwards, his body was hung up in chains at Gun Cay as a warning to those who dared defy the law.

# BLACK BART

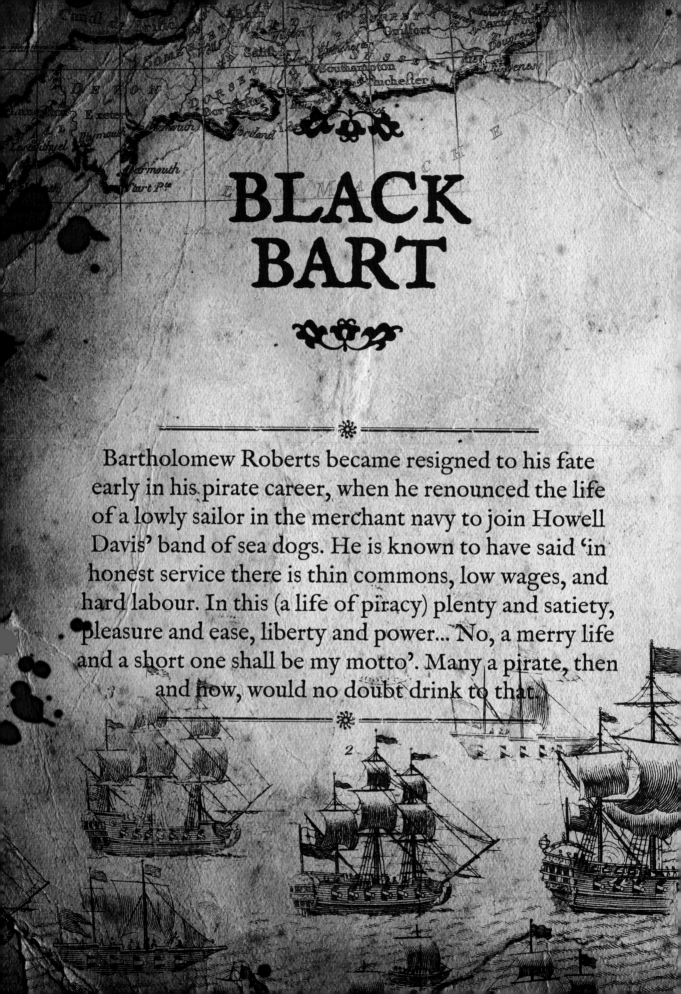

Bartholomew Roberts became resigned to his fate early in his pirate career, when he renounced the life of a lowly sailor in the merchant navy to join Howell Davis' band of sea dogs. He is known to have said 'in honest service there is thin commons, low wages, and hard labour. In this (a life of piracy) plenty and satiety, pleasure and ease, liberty and power... No, a merry life and a short one shall be my motto'. Many a pirate, then and now, would no doubt drink to that.

Captain Kidd and Blackbeard are probably the most famous pirates of all time. But the pirate who was the most successful, with a staggering total of 470 captured ships to his name, was a Welshman named John Roberts. Early in his career, Roberts adopted the name Bartholomew, but it was only after his death that he came to be known as Black Bart, a reference not just to his dark eyes and hair, but to his devilish soul.

## A NAVAL 'TAR'

John Roberts was born in 1682, the son of George Roberts and his wife, who lived in the village of Little Newcastle – *Casnewydd Bach* in Welsh - near the seaside town of Fishguard in West Wales. The area was a Welsh-speaking one, and Roberts grew up with Welsh as his first language. This was later to prove useful when he met the pirate captain Howell Davis, and the pair were able to converse in Welsh without the other pirates knowing what they were talking about.

At the age of 13, young John decided to become a sailor, and joined the merchant navy. Once there, he soon became acquainted with the miserable pay and conditions. However, undeterred, he quickly learned the ropes, and soon became an extremely skilled seaman, showing a particular flair for navigation. But there was little chance of promotion for an ordinary sailor like him, and he soon realized that if he stayed in the navy, he was going to have to work for a pittance.

## A MERRY LIFE AND A SHORT ONE

In 1719, Roberts found himself aboard the *Princess*, whose cargo was live human beings – slaves. While the boat was at anchor off the Cold Coast of West Africa, it was attacked by pirates, led by one Captain Davis. The crew were captured and forced to join the pirate band. Initially, Roberts was less than enthusiastic about his new situation, but after a while, it became clear to him that he had fallen into a better way of life. According to Captain Johnson's report of him, he reasoned that, 'in honest service there is thin commons, low wages, and hard labour. In this, plenty and satiety, pleasure and ease, liberty and power … No, a merry life and a short one shall be my motto'.

On becoming a pirate, Roberts changed his name, becoming Bartholomew Roberts (the name may have been inspired by a notorious English buccaneer, Bartholomew Sharp). The new recruit soon became a favourite with Captain Davis, not only because he hailed from the same area in West Wales, but because he proved to be an excellent navigator. He was also, as it transpired, a courageous fighter and a merciless disciplinarian, able to command respect from the drunken, rowdy bunch of thieves and vagabonds who made up the crew.

## BLOODY REVENGE

Hoisting a British flag, the pirates made their way to Principe, Portugal, where they posed as naval officers and were lavishly entertained by the Portuguese Governor. Davis then plotted to kidnap the Governor, but his plan was discovered. The Governor invited Davis and his men to call on him for drinks and ambushed them as they made their way to his house. Davis took a bullet through the stomach and died an agonizing death, firing his pistols as he took his last breath.

The pirates fled, regrouped and decided to make Roberts their captain. He accepted, reflecting that 'since he had dipped his hands in muddy water and must be a pirate, it was better being a commander than a common man'.

On taking over command, Roberts' first action was to return to Principe, bombard the fort, kill all the male inhabitants and ransack the town, in revenge for Davis' killing. He then set sail for Brazil, attacking some slave ships on the way, until he came upon the Lisbon fleet. Although there were over 40 ships in the fleet, some of them heavily armed, Roberts managed to rob the richest of them and sail away with a heap of gold coins and jewellery worth thousands of pounds.

## THE BLACK FLAG

Soon after, however, one of Roberts' deputies ran off with one of his ships, leaving him in the lurch. In response, Roberts issued an edict to all his men to the effect that if any of them ever robbed him again, they would have their nose and ears slit. He also made a number of other rules, such as forbidding robbery and gambling and warning that any pirate found guilty of rape would be put to death. In a rare moment of kindness, he also ruled that pirates who lost a limb in the course of their duties should receive compensation of 'eight hundred pieces of eight from the common stock.'

Before long, Roberts was back in action attacking shipping around Martinique and Barbados. His reputation as a merciless pirate was enhanced when, in one instance, he hanged the Governor of Martinique from the yardarm of his ship. He then moved on to Senegal and Sierra Leone, plundering slave ships, so terrorizing them that when they saw his flag, they immediately surrendered. Fully aware of the power of self-promotion, Roberts had several black flags made, one showing him standing by a death's head with an hourglass, and another of him with his feet planted on two skulls labelled AMH and ABH – a Martiniquan and a Barbadian.

## SUDDEN DEATH

By this stage in his career, Roberts was obviously enjoying his life as a pirate. He dressed in glamorous clothes stolen from the treasure ships. A tall, dark-haired man, he wore red damask waistcoats and breeches, a red feather in his hat, a diamond and gold necklace and ornamented pistols and swords. However, his liking for finery did not alter his behaviour as a captain: he remained a skilful sailor, a gifted strategist, a courageous fighter and a strict disciplinarian. Unlike many pirate captains of the day, he planned his attacks in minute detail, and was able to keep order among his men, which may have been why he was so much more successful than the rest of the freebooters. Certainly, the fact that he disliked drunkenness, and is said to have preferred to drink tea rather than beer, must have helped him to keep a clear head.

However, even the best pirate captain could not stop his crew from drinking, especially from carousing when they had just ransacked a ship, and this is what eventually proved to be his undoing. On 10 February 1722, a naval ship, the HMS *Swallow*, chased Roberts' ship and shot at it. Roberts, standing on deck in his finery, was killed instantly. As the battle raged, the shocked crew – determined not to deliver him to the enemy – wrapped up his body in the ship's sail, weighed it down, and threw it overboard. It sank into the depths, and never resurfaced.

Roberts had envisaged that he would end up on the gibbet, but in the event, his death was a sudden one, aboard his own ship, in battle. Undoubtedly, it was what he would have chosen for himself. Afterwards, he became a legendary figure as Black Bart, the most successful pirate of his generation.

This 18th century engraving shows Black Bart with
two ships, the *Royal Fortune* and *Ranger*, as they set sail
on the coast of Guinea.

# CALICO JACK, ANNE BONNEY & MARY READ

Together Calico Jack, Anne Bonney and Mary Read were a force to be reckoned with in the early part of the 18th century. Each brought something different to the table; Jack — the dandily dressed, slightly cowardly, pirate captain, Anne — his fearsome lover, who could fight courageously and competently against any man — and Mary, the cross-dressing pirate who wore her heart on her sleeve. It is no wonder that this band of misfit ruffians continue to fascinate us to this day.

One of the most flamboyant pirates to ply his trade in the Spanish Main was Calico Jack, so called because of the brightly coloured printed cotton clothes he liked to wear. He was not a particularly successful pirate, mostly limiting his operations to attacking small ships, but he has remained legendary, not only because of his striking appearance but because he employed two female pirates in his crew: Anne Bonney and Mary Read.

Calico Jack is also credited with being one of the first pirates to fly the Jolly Roger, featuring a skull and crossed cutlasses. This popular design later mutated into the skull and crossbones, and has become forever associated with piracy.

## PREYING ON THE WEAK

Calico Jack's real name was John Rackham. He was born in England on 21 December 1682. There is no further mention of him in the records of the period until 1718, when he found employment as quartermaster for the pirate Charles Vane (see page 46). Vane mostly preyed on weaker vessels, but in one instance he attacked a ship that turned out to be a French man of war, and had to retreat, much to the humiliation of his crew. The crew turned on Vane, called him a coward, and voted that Rackham should take his place as captain. So it was that Calico Jack came to command his first ship.

As a pirate, Rackham's career was somewhat undistinguished. He patrolled the coastline close to the shore, and often chose to attack small fishing boats, terrifying ordinary men and women as they went about their work. He was not known for his bravery in battle, either: one story goes that he gave up his stolen ship without a fight when its Jamaican owner reclaimed it, and retired to New Providence Island in the Bahamas. At the time, the island was known as a meeting point for pirates from all over the world. Once there, he received a pardon from the Governor of the Bahamas, Woodes Rogers.

## SIZEABLE FORTUNE

But Rackham's retirement did not last long. He frequented the taverns in the island's main town, Nassau, meeting the pirates who gathered there to hatch plots and launch operations. In the course of his socializing, he met a notorious firebrand, a local woman named Anne Bonney, and began a passionate affair with her. Anne was married, and at first the affair was conducted in secret. However, it was not long before the lovers became careless, and Anne's husband found out what was going on. After a major scandal, Jack and Anne eloped together and ran away to sea, thus escaping Anne's belligerent husband and the long arm of the law.

Once at sea, Jack reverted to his old ways as a pirate, and Anne began, literally, to learn the ropes. For the next year or so, Jack, Anne, and their pirate band plied their trade around the islands of the Caribbean, attacking small ships and amassing a sizeable fortune for themselves. In the course of their adventures, they encountered a privateer ship, attacked it, and came upon Mary Read, a female pirate who dressed as a man. Bored with life on the legal side of sea robbery, Mary decided to switch allegiance, and joined Calico Jack's pirate crew. Once the new recruit was on-board, Anne, who by all accounts had a healthy sexual appetite, was immediately attracted to the young sailor. Jack became jealous, but when Mary revealed her secret – that she was, in fact, a woman – Jack was happy to allow her to stay on-board, work

RIGHT: Calico Jack, Anne Bonney and Mary Read in the Antilles.

among the men, and keep his wife company. Mary and Anne subsequently went on to become firm friends.

## GRUESOME WARNING

However, this cosy set-up was not to last. Unbeknown to Calico Jack, time was running out for his pirate band. The Governor, Woodes Rogers, had come under public pressure to do something about the escalating levels of piracy in the Caribbean, which was adversely affecting trade in and around the islands there. He decided to begin his clean-up campaign by focusing on his old adversary, Calico Jack.

Once he learned that Jack had broken the conditions of the pardon and returned to piracy, Woodes sent a force to capture him. In October 1720, a sloop commanded by Captain Jonathan Barnet caught up with the pirates in Jamaica, attacking the ship as the crew lay drunk after a night of revelry. The ship was overtaken, the crew arrested, and the entire company taken to Spanish Town, Jamaica to await trial.

Not surprisingly, given the fact that there were two women pirates in the dock, the trial of Calico Jack and his crew caused tremendous public interest. Jack was the first to be found guilty, and was immediately sentenced to death. He was hanged on 18 November 1720. His body was then covered in tar, placed in a cage and hung on a gibbet on an island outside Port Royal, Jamaica, as a gruesome warning to other pirates. The island is now known as Rackham's Cay. The nine men in his crew were tried the following year and were also sentenced to death. They were hanged in February 1721.

The women, however, escaped the noose. Both Anne Bonney and Mary Read announced that they were pregnant, which meant that under the law they could not be hanged until after they had given birth. But as it turned out, they never were hanged: in the event, Mary Read died of a fever related to her condition, while Anne Bonney disappeared from the records.

Today, Calico Jack is remembered as the gaudily dressed pirate who sailed the high seas with two females in his crew, flying the Jolly Roger in a gesture of defiance to the law of the land.

## ANNE BONNEY

The story of Anne Bonney is one of passion, violence and adventure. Of Irish-American extraction, she was one of very few women to go down in history as a female pirate. (Another was her friend, Mary Read, whose story you can read below.) She was renowned for her volatile temper, her courage and her prowess as a fighter. She survived many skirmishes at sea, but was eventually imprisoned. However, in the end she managed to escape the hangman's noose, whether through luck or cunning we do not know.

### VIOLENT TEMPER

There are few official records concerning Anne Bonney's early years. Most of what we know about her comes from Captain Charles Johnson's *A General History of the Pyrates*, published in 1724 and thought by some to be the work of Daniel Defoe. Johnson writes that Bonney was born near Cork, Ireland, the illegitimate daughter of a well-to-do lawyer named William Cormac and his maidservant, whose surname was Brennan. After the baby was born, the couple moved to Charleston, Carolina, to avoid scandal, Miss Brennan posing as his wife. There,

Cormac amassed a fortune and went on to buy a plantation.

When Anne's mother died, Anne kept house for her father, and by all accounts grew to be a violently bad-tempered young person. Aged only 13, she was reputed to have stabbed a servant girl with a kitchen knife. It was also rumoured that on one occasion she rebuffed an unfortunate young man's advances by giving him a thorough beating for his pains.

By the time she reached adulthood, Anne had developed a taste for excitement and adventure. Against her father's wishes, she married a disreputable sailor, James Bonney, and moved to Nassau, New Providence. There, her new husband immediately made himself unpopular by becoming a paid informer to the governor of the Bahamas, Woodes Rogers.

## PUBLIC FLOGGING

The Bonneys' marriage was not a success. When Anne realized that her husband was an informer, and had only married her to get his hands on her father's estate, she took to going out by herself, frequenting the local inns and mixing with the pirates there. When she began an affair with the notorious Calico Jack, her husband was outraged, and brought her before Governor Rogers, demanding that the Governor order a public flogging for her. Rogers suggested that, instead, James might like to make some kind of divorce settlement, which would involve him 'selling' his wife to her new lover, in a practice that was common at the time. Avaricious as ever, Anne's husband jumped at the chance. Anne, however, put up a spirited resistance to the idea, refusing to take part in the deal, and protesting that she would not be 'bought and sold like cattle'. Rogers duly ordered the flogging, but before it could take place, Jack and Anne had fled the island.

Johnson recounts how, once at sea, Anne took to wearing men's clothes to disguise herself. However, this is disputed by some historians, who point to a circular printed in the *Boston Newsletter* at the time, which specifically names her as a 'wanted pirate'. This suggests that she was well known to be female, and did not try to hide the fact. Nevertheless, she did gain a reputation as a woman who was as tough, or tougher, than any man: on-board ship, she proved both a competent sailor and a courageous fighter.

## THE PREGNANT PIRATE

Before long, however, Anne became pregnant, and it looked for a time as though she would have to retire from life as a sea robber to take up the responsibilities of motherhood on shore. But instead, Rackham merely dropped her off with friends in Cuba, waited until she had had the baby, and then picked her up again, leaving the child to be brought up by the ever-obliging friends. Lacking a maternal streak, Anne seemed happy with the arrangement, returning to pirate life with gusto.

## HANGED LIKE A DOG

Despite her notoriety, Bonney never commanded her own ship. That duty was always left to her lover, Calico Jack. But it might have been better if she had, since when Governor Rogers finally sent a naval posse to capture them, it was Bonney, along with her friend Read, who fought manfully to evade capture while Jack and his men lay drunk and incapable below deck. When the crew were finally taken prisoner, Anne was apparently furious at Jack's behaviour. The story goes that when she visited her lover in jail, instead of commiserating with him, she told him, 'I am sorry to see you here, Jack, but if you had fought like a man, you would not be hanged like a dog'.

While Anne was in jail, it transpired that she was again pregnant, which this time proved extremely fortunate for her. She was able to obtain a stay of execution from the judge, who ordered that she could not be hanged until after her baby was born. (English law maintained that a condemned woman, if pregnant, should not be put to death until after childbirth, so that the baby would survive.)

## MYSTERIOUS DISAPPEARANCE

Strangely, however, at this point Anne Bonney completely disappeared from the historical record. There is no documentation of her execution, and many believe that it never happened. It is argued that, had she been executed, the matter would have been noted down, whether in prison records or in the press, since she was a female pirate of such notoriety. So what could have happened to her? To this day, nobody really knows.

Some believe her wealthy father ransomed her; others that she returned home to her husband; still others that she went on to pursue a life of piracy under another name. There is also a theory, put forward by her descendents, that she married a Charleston man, Joseph Burleigh, and went on to raise a family of nine children, including her second child by Calico Jack. According to this claim, Anne lived to a ripe old age – with more than a few wild stories of her youth to tell her grandchildren, no doubt – until her death on 25 April 1782 at the age of 82 .

## MARY READ

The image of the cross-dressing female pirate is one that has always intrigued and delighted the public. Yet it appears that, of the small band of female pirates that existed in the 18th century, very few actually dressed as men. Mary Read was an exception: she really did cross-dress, and has gone down in history as the swashbuckling pirate with a secret to hide: that she was, in fact, a woman.

Read was born in London to a sea captain and his wife, who decided to bring their daughter up as a boy. Accounts vary as to why. Some suggest that the couple's first child had indeed been a boy, but that he had died while an infant, and that the mother had then had an affair while the sea captain was away, resulting in Mary's birth. When the captain did not return, the wife dressed the child in boy's clothes and went to visit her wealthy mother-in-law, claiming that he was the son, and so managed to get an allowance for them. Others claim that Mary's mother simply dressed her daughter as a boy because she thought that it would be good for her to have all the privileges of a man when she became an adult.

## BRAVE SOLDIER

In her teenage years, Mary found employment as a footboy to a wealthy French family living in London. However, she hated being a servant, so she decided to run away to sea. She joined a warship, but soon realized that she had made a mistake. For several years she endured the miserable conditions on-board ship, before joining the army. She became a foot soldier at the lowest rank, but showed such bravery at the Battle of Flanders that she was promoted to the cavalry. During this time, she met a soldier and fell in love with him. When she revealed that

she was a woman, he offered to marry her, and the pair left the army to become civilians.

Mary and her new husband went on to run an inn, The Three Horseshoes. The inn prospered, and for a while, she lived contentedly in her new role as pub landlady, dressing as a woman for the first time in her life. However, her happiness was not to last. When her husband died, she donned her man's clothes once more, left the inn, and went back to the army. She then joined the crew of a privateer vessel sailing to the Spanish Main. When the ship was attacked by pirates, she was held prisoner.

## PASSION AND DANGER

Her captors turned out to be Calico Jack and his mistress Anne Bonney. Anne immediately took a fancy to Mary, thinking her to be a man. Whether they had a sexual relationship or not remains unclear – some reports suggest that Calico Jack found the two of them in his bed together – but whatever happened, Mary's secret came out.

Read then joined the pirate crew, making friends with Anne, and fighting side by side with the men as they robbed and plundered cargo ships in the Caribbean. Of a passionate nature, she fell madly in love with a young sailor, and when he was in danger, offered to lay down her life for him. The sailor had been challenged to a duel by an older and much stronger seaman, so Mary decided to take the young man's place. She and the seaman fought fiercely, with pistols and swords, until at one point he made a lunge at her. So as to confuse him, she ripped open her shirt, revealing her breasts, and as he reeled back in surprise, she stabbed him to death.

## REBEL SPIRIT

Mary and the young sailor celebrated this triumph by getting married, but once again domestic bliss was to elude her. Shortly after the nuptials, Calico Jack and his crew were captured,

imprisoned, and sentenced to death. Mary was found to be pregnant, and thus escaped execution, only to die of a fever soon afterwards. Her unborn child perished with her.

Today, she is remembered as one of the most intriguing pirates of the 18th century. Despite her reputation as a tough soldier, a bloodthirsty pirate and a brave fighter, she also had a reputation as a tender-hearted woman in her personal life. She was prone to falling in love, and to forming intense friendships, and when she did, treated the objects of her affection with great loyalty and devotion. She was also admired for her courage; she was not intimidated by the punishment for piracy, which was the death sentence, and once remarked, 'As to hanging, it is no great hardship. For were it not for that, every cowardly fellow would turn pirate and so unfit the sea, that men of courage must starve.'

Like many other pirates of the day, Mary Read appears to have lived by her own moral code, which valued honour and bravery in battle, and personal loyalty to those she loved. She was part of a renegade band of outcasts: some were from poverty-stricken backgrounds who had been hounded by the law for various misdemeanours, while others came from wealthier stock but had flouted the rules of social convention in one way or another. Despite, or perhaps because of, their rejection from polite society, these individuals nevertheless formed strong alliances with each other, and were a great deal more tolerant of deviation from the norm, whether physical, moral or social, than the general public of the period. Thus, although the pirates were feared, they were also, to some extent, admired and envied.

Women like Mary Read, who were not afraid to live a life of passion, independence and self-determination, just as men did, were especially few and far between. These were the rebels, who refused to slot into the roles prescribed for them, as dutiful daughters, wives and mothers. Such women were as unusual then as they are now; and for this reason, to this day, they continue to fascinate us.

LEFT: Mary Read fights a pirate to save her lover's life.

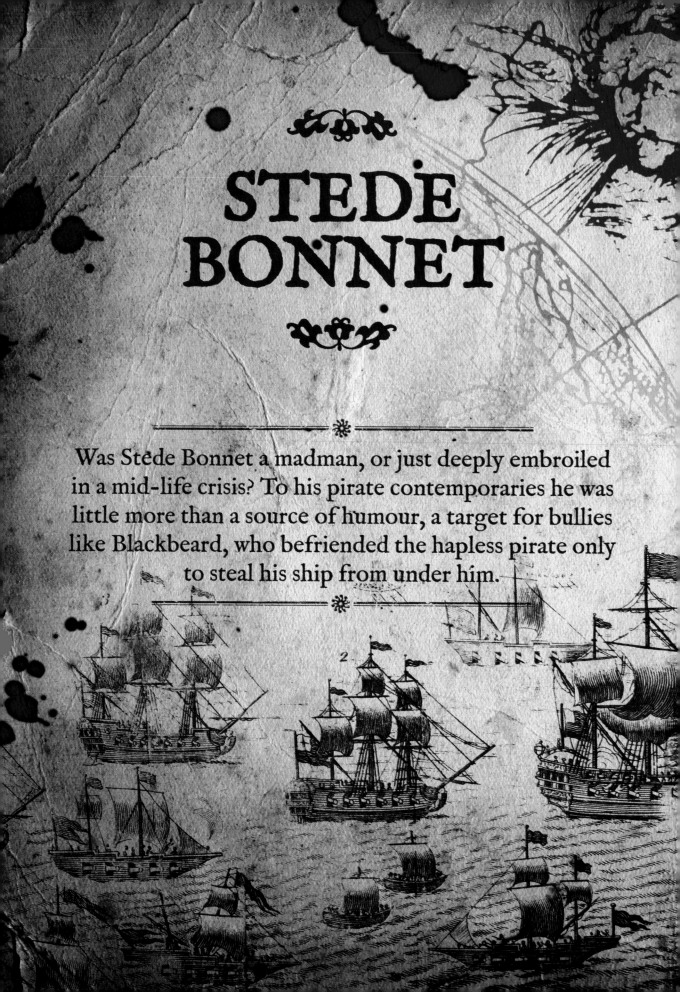

# STEDE BONNET

Was Stede Bonnet a madman, or just deeply embroiled in a mid-life crisis? To his pirate contemporaries he was little more than a source of humour, a target for bullies like Blackbeard, who befriended the hapless pirate only to steal his ship from under him.

Stede Bonnet was one of the strangest pirates in history. Unlike his peers, he was not driven to piracy through poverty and ill fortune. Quite the contrary: at the time he decided to take to a life of crime on the high seas, he was a well-to-do, middle-aged man with a wife and children. Yet, for reasons that are still unclear, he decided to quit his comfortable life as a wealthy plantation owner on the island of Barbados and instead seek his fortune by robbery and murder at sea.

## MID-LIFE CRISIS?

Bonnet was born in Barbados in 1688, the son of a rich landowner. When his father died, he inherited the family estate, and married a young woman, Mary Allamby, who bore him three sons and a daughter. As a young man he enjoyed studying, and was known for his bookish nature. He joined the Barbadian militia, whose main function was to quell slave riots, and rose to the rank of major before retiring in middle age to manage his estate.

It was after a few years of retirement that, quite unexpectedly, without the knowledge of his family or social circle, he suddenly took it into his head to run off and become a pirate. Whether this was because of marital difficulties – it was rumoured that his wife nagged him mercilessly – or because he was bored with his pleasant, comfortable life on the estate, is not known. Some believe that Bonnet may have suffered from mental illness, and certainly, his later antics during his career as a pirate would warrant such an explanation. Today, we would perhaps be tempted to describe his action as a 'mid-life crisis'. But whatever it was, there is no doubt that it resulted in a very bad outcome for all concerned, not least Bonnet himself, who was eventually hanged for his crimes.

## OFF-THE-PEG PIRACY

Instead of stealing a ship, as most pirates did, Bonnet went out and bought one. It was a well-appointed, 60 ton sloop, which he named the *Revenge*. He was a rich man, and he could well afford such an extravagance. He moored the ship in the local harbour, and proceeded to equip it with six guns. No one understood why he was doing this, and the ship remained in the harbour for several days, the subject of much speculation. Meanwhile, Bonnet was busy assembling a crew for his new enterprise.

This way of embarking on a life of piracy was unheard of, and caused a great deal of amusement within the pirate community. Rather than drawing a band of pirates around him through his reputation as a leader who could loot ships effectively, and was known to divide his spoils fairly between his men, Bonnet simply went out and offered to hire his crew, promising to pay them regular weekly wages. Furthermore, he admitted that he knew nothing about boats or sailing whatsoever and would be relying on his men to advise him what to do.

Not surprisingly, he received very little respect from the sailors, and many of them treated him with derision. However, they were attracted to the steady income that he promised to provide, and so it was that, in the end, 70 experienced seamen signed up to sail on the new ship.

Bonnet and his pirate band sailed out of Carlisle Bay, Barbados, under cover of darkness one night. He left his home, his family, and all his friends without telling a soul. Bonnet's life as a pirate had begun.

Despite his initial inexperience, he somehow managed to rob several ships off the coasts of Virginia, the Carolinas and New York, relying on the skill of the sailors under his command. He always took care to burn any Barbadian ships, in case news of his crimes reached home. This again marked him out from most pirates, who could not have cared less what their families and friends back home thought of their behaviour.

## Blackbeard 'Befriends' him

In 1717, the *Revenge* was attacked by an armed Spanish ship, and Bonnet lost half of his crew. He escaped, badly wounded, and retired to the island of Nassau, a well-known pirate hideout at the time, to reassemble his crew and make repairs. While recuperating there, he met the notorious pirate Blackbeard.

The two men initially got on well. Blackbeard was impressed by Bonnet's genteel manners while Bonnet, for his part, was awed by Blackbeard's charisma and the fear he inspired in his men. However, the relationship soon turned sour. It soon became clear that Blackbeard was a ruthless opportunist, who had only befriended the hapless Bonnet to take advantage of him.

It was not long before Blackbeard lured away Bonnet's entire crew, took control of his ship, added it to his fleet, and began to mount attacks on passing merchant ships. Bonnet felt utterly betrayed, but there was nothing he could do about it. He was left to while away his time as a 'guest' – or as he described it, a prisoner – on-board his own ship. According to some reports, he often walked up and down the deck in his nightgown, incapable of doing anything but watching the various battles as they raged around him.

## Facing the gallows

After the Blockade of Charleston, Blackbeard's fortunes waned, but he was able to gain a pardon from the Governor of North Carolina. Bonnet was pardoned too, on condition that he did not return to piracy. Although the pirates' activities were clearly a menace to law and order, the authorities were keen to keep them sweet and engage them as privateers in the War of Spanish Secession that was being waged at the time. Unfortunately though, pirates were not known for keeping their word, and in no time both Blackbeard and Bonnet were back to their old ways, robbing ordinary merchant vessels instead of armed Spanish warships.

Bonnet's ship, now renamed *Royal James*, cruised along the Virginia Coast. Over the years, he had become more adept at plundering civilian vessels, along with others such as Charles Vane. Piracy was becoming a severe problem in the Caribbean, and the public were pressing the authorities to take action. Accordingly, they hired a local ship owner, William Rhett, to find and capture the pirates. Rhett chose two sloops, the *Henry* and the *Sea Nymph* to do the job. They were led, respectively, by Captain Masters and Captain Hall, and each commanded upwards of 50 men.

The captains tracked Bonnet's ship down to a mooring on the Cape Fear River, and on 27 September 1718, engaged him in battle. After five hours of fighting, Bonnet was captured. In October, he was taken to Charleston and imprisoned. However, on 24 October he escaped, but was later recaptured, and sent to trial, where Judge Nicholas Trott issued him with a death sentence. Bonnet begged for mercy, offering to cut off both his arms and legs so that he would have no possibility of returning to a life of piracy. The Governor was moved by this plea, remarking that Bonnet's mind was clearly disordered, but after delaying his execution several times, he finally gave the order. On 10 December 1718, Stede Bonnet was hanged.

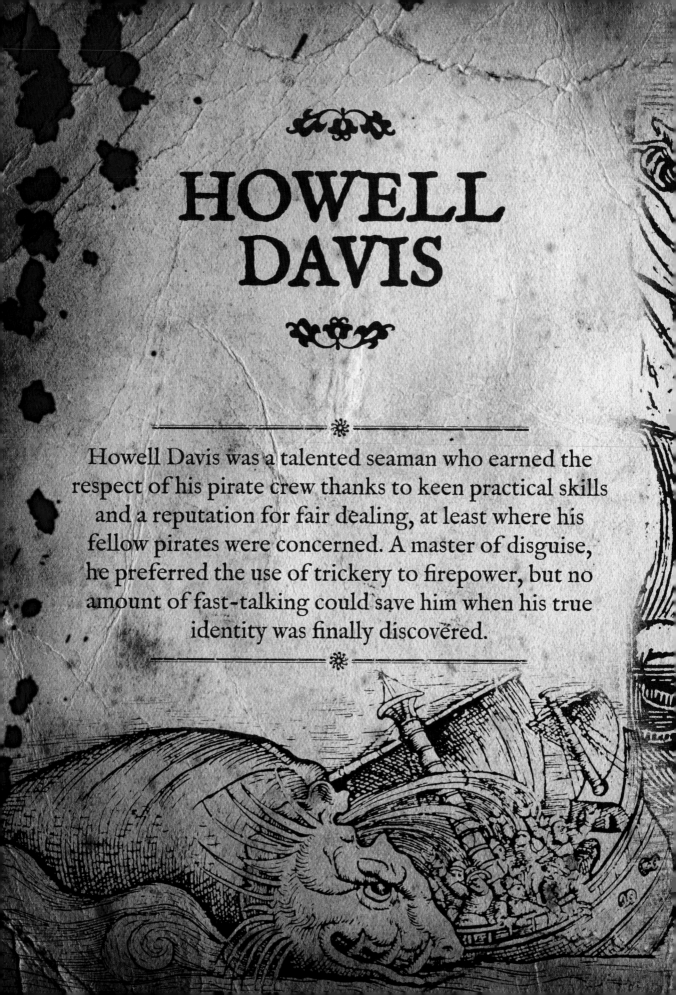

# HOWELL DAVIS

Howell Davis was a talented seaman who earned the respect of his pirate crew thanks to keen practical skills and a reputation for fair dealing, at least where his fellow pirates were concerned. A master of disguise, he preferred the use of trickery to firepower, but no amount of fast-talking could save him when his true identity was finally discovered.

owell Davis was a Welsh pirate whose career lasted only 11 months, from July 1718 to June 1719. No matter how short-lived his piratical spree, Davis seems to have embraced a life of crime on the high seas with real enthusiasm. Davis was a clever and charming man who enjoyed a favourable reputation as a generous and humane person. He preferred to use trickery and disguise in order to achieve his aims rather than violence, but he was also impulsive, and tended to act first and think later, a weakness that would land him at the centre of one scrape after another.

Howell Davis was born in Milford Haven in Pembrokeshire, Wales, sometime around the year 1690. He ran away to join the crew of a slaving ship – the *Cadogan* – at a very young age, and worked his way up to the position of first mate. In the summer of 1718, the *Cadogan* was attacked and captured by the Irish pirate Edward England off the West African coast. England shared Davis' aversion to violence, and had a reputation for showing extraordinary mercy toward his captives. In fact, his crew eventually mutinied against him for refusing to kill captives from the ship the *Cassandra*, and he was marooned on Mauritius for his efforts, so it is doubtful that Davis was forced, on pain of death, to turn pirate. It is much more likely that Davis was impressed by England and welcomed the opportunity to participate in some adventure. He must have shown real skill, not to mention enthusiasm for this new life, because England gave him command of the *Cadogan* almost immediately, and they set sail for Brazil, where he planned to sell the ship.

The crew, it seemed, were not as enamoured with Davis' style of leadership. They wanted to keep the ship and decided instead to sail for Barbados and dispose of their cargo, where they were captured and imprisoned on suspicion of piracy. Davis spent three months behind bars, but managed, somewhat surprisingly, to escape sentencing. We do not know whether this was due to lack of evidence, or personal charm, but in

those lawless days a resounding lack of evidence rarely deterred the courts from convicting anyone of any crime they pleased, so one must conclude that Davis' winning character had more to do with him regaining his freedom.

On release from prison Davis' first destination was New Providence, in the Bahamas. However, he soon regretted this decision when he discovered that the new governor there, Woodes Rogers, had taken a staunchly anti-pirate stance and was in the process of clamping down. He chose instead to sail for the West Indies aboard the *Buck*, a sloop crewed by many of Rogers' own men. Once at Martinique, Davis conspired with six other members of the crew and managed to raise a mutiny. Davis was promptly elected captain, and set about conducting piratical raids from a base in Coxon Hole, before crossing the Atlantic to terrorize shipping off the Cape Verde Islands. It was here that Davis stumbled upon and captured the ship that was to head-up his pirate fleet – the 26-gun *Saint James*.

Once in Cape Verde, Davis underwent something of a makeover. He began to dress as a dandy and to pose as an English privateer rather than a common-or-garden pirate, taking full advantage of the local Portuguese governor's generosity before setting sail for St Maio, where he plundered many ships and recruited many more men. It was under this guise that Davis and two of his trusty crew mates went to the Royal

Africa's Fort on the Gambia River, where the governor invited them to dinner. At the feast, their host was taken prisoner and relieved of £2,000 in gold.

Around this time Davis met and became closely associated with two other pirate captains. The first was Olivier La Bouche, a Frenchman who, like Davis, had also fled New Providence in the wake of Woodes Rogers political war on piracy. La Bouche first encountered Davis and his men whilst they were celebrating the sacking of the Fort at Gambia. Davis' crew spotted a ship bearing down on them in full sail, and were hastily preparing to fight her when she ran up the black flag. On closer inspection the approaching ship proved to be a French pirate ship of 14 guns and 64 hands, half French in origin and half African. The two captains agreed to sail down the coast together, and when they arrived at Sierra Leone they came across a tall ship lying at anchor, which they attacked with a broadside. This ship also turned out to be a pirate ship, captained this time by an Englishman, Thomas Cocklyn, who was also in the process of escaping from New Providence. The three captains entered into an agreement to join forces and work the seas together, but the relationship proved to be booze-fuelled and tumultuous. They captured a West Africa-bound slave ship, the *Bird Galley*, at the mouth of Sierra Leone River, and celebrated their victory on-board for nearly an entire month before finally releasing her captain, William Snelgrave, giving him the *Bristol Snow* as well as any meagre cargo they had left following the crew's occupation of the ship. The three captains' working relationship came to an end when a drunken argument, over what to do next, put paid to any talk of further cooperation between them or their men.

When the pirate cooperative parted company, Davis seized four large English and Dutch ships loaded with gold, ivory and slaves. He exchanged the *Buck* for a 32-gun ship which he renamed the *Rover*, before successfully capturing three more British slave ships. It was on one of these ships that Davis met a young man named Bartholomew Roberts, who was to become known as the notorious Black Bart, scourge of the seven seas.

It seemed as if the career of Captain Davis was just hitting its stride, but then things took a turn for the worse. He and his crew sailed for Principe, a small island off the West coast of Africa, where he posed, not as a privateer, but as a pirate hunter, even going so far as to seize a French ship as it was coming into harbour because he claimed it had been trading with pirates. Davis had hatched a plan to kidnap the Portuguese governor of the Island, and was on his way to dine with him when the governor's guards, who must somehow have figured out his real identity, ambushed and killed him. Davis was able to draw his pistols and kill two of his attackers as he bled to death, but that was not enough for his crew. They wanted real revenge and under the leadership of his prodigy, Bartholomew Roberts, they burnt the Governor's fort and shelled the town in retaliation. Proving that Howell Davis was a tremendously well-liked pirate captain, a man who managed to command a great deal of loyalty from his men even in death.

RIGHT: An illustration depicting the death of Howell Davis.

# JOHN GOW

As a pirate captain, John Gow, or 'The Orkney Pirate' as he became known, showed little promise, and he has gone down in history as something of a bungler. Nevertheless he managed to terrorize the inhabitants of many large mansions on his boyhood home of Orkney, where he will be remembered as a villain, nothing more and nothing less.

John Gow, also known as 'The Orkney Pirate', had a short career characterized, at the end, by bumbling incompetence. Like fellow adventurers Richard Coyle and John Richardson, he is remembered today for his failure rather than his success.

Gow was born in Wick, Scotland, in 1698. His father William was a merchant. At some point in his childhood, the family moved to Stromness in the Orkney Islands, where he attended school. Some reports suggest that, while still in his teens, he ran away to sea, but the first time he appeared in the annals of history was when he turned pirate in the summer of 1724, aged 26.

## MUTINY AND MURDER

The ship he was working on, the *Caroline*, was a trading vessel plying routes between such ports as Amsterdam, Genoa and Santa Cruz. At Santa Cruz, the ship came to a halt and there was a long delay before the next passage. For two months, the crew waited in the port, growing ever more restless. Gow's post on the ship was as second mate and gunner, a relatively senior position. So when the crew began to complain about the dreadful food and conditions, Gow was the person they turned to.

The captain of the ship was a Frenchman named Ferneau. Realizing the fact that he was in danger, Ferneau armed himself and his small band of officers, so that any uprising could be contained. However, the unrest grew steadily worse until the crew finally carried out a mutiny. In the middle of the night, they crept into the cabins of the officers and cut their throats. One of the officers, a surgeon, managed to stagger up onto the deck to get help from the captain. However, he died before anything could be done for him. The captain was then set upon by several men, but fought bravely against them, only to be finished off with a bullet from the gun of John Gow. After shooting Ferneau, Gow threw his

body overboard, and the crew hastily sailed away. The *Caroline* was renamed the *Revenge*, and the sailors on it became pirates overnight.

## ROBBERY AND RAPE

For several years, Gow and his men preyed on shipping around the coasts of Portugal, France and Spain. They made a reasonable living, and achieved a certain level of notoriety, but eventually, their luck began to run out. So Gow had a brainwave. He remembered that there were many large mansions on his boyhood home of Orkney, most of them owned by absent landlords. He conceived a plan to rob them. Unfortunately for him, the plan was less than perfect.

Arriving in the Orkneys, Gow and his men posed as respectable merchants. Gow came up with a story that he had been sailing his ship on a trade route from Stockholm to Cadiz when he encountered a fierce storm and was blown off course. He added that he had grown up in Stromness, and was now visiting his childhood home after the traumatic experience of almost being shipwrecked. Gow renamed himself 'Mr Smith' and his ship the *George*, and for a few weeks, he and his men remained in the town, enjoying the convivial life of the taverns there.

However, it was not long before the townspeople began to suspect that Mr Smith was not the honest merchant that he claimed to be. As his ship lay in dock, a visiting merchant passed by and recognized it as the pirate ship the *Revenge*. The merchant also recognized some of Gow's crewmen, and actually managed to persuade one of them to jump ship. Others, sensing danger, sailed off to Scotland in one of the small boats belonging to the *Revenge*.

## Execution Dock

It was then that Gow made his first foray into housebreaking. He and his remaining men robbed the Hall of Clestrain, a large mansion belonging to one Robert Honeyman. Terrifying Honeyman's wife and daughter, he made off with silver and other valuables, allegedly abducting and raping two servant girls. Next, he set his sights on Carrick House, home of a former school friend, James Fea. However, on the way, his ship ran aground at the Calf of

Eday, not far from the house. Fea then alerted the authorities, who arrived and arrested the gang. They were taken to England and sent to Marshalsea Prison in London to await trial.

All the pirates were sentenced to death, and were hanged at Execution Dock on the Thames on 11 June 1725. The *Newgate Calendar* relates that Gow did not die immediately. To ease his passing, friends pulled at his legs, but this broke the rope he was hanging from, which meant that the whole grisly procedure had to be started again from the beginning. Afterwards, the bodies of Gow and his men were tarred and strung up on the riverbank.

# KANHOJI ANGRE

The inclusion of Kanhoji Angre in the pirate section of this book is controversial, since he is widely regarded as a hero in his native country. The line between pirate and privateer is an extremely thin one, and most of the men and women in this book spent the majority of their days with a foot on each side of the fence. Angre was no exception, to some he was a saviour, a defender of the realm and to others a villainous ruffian, a thorn in the side of the East India Company.

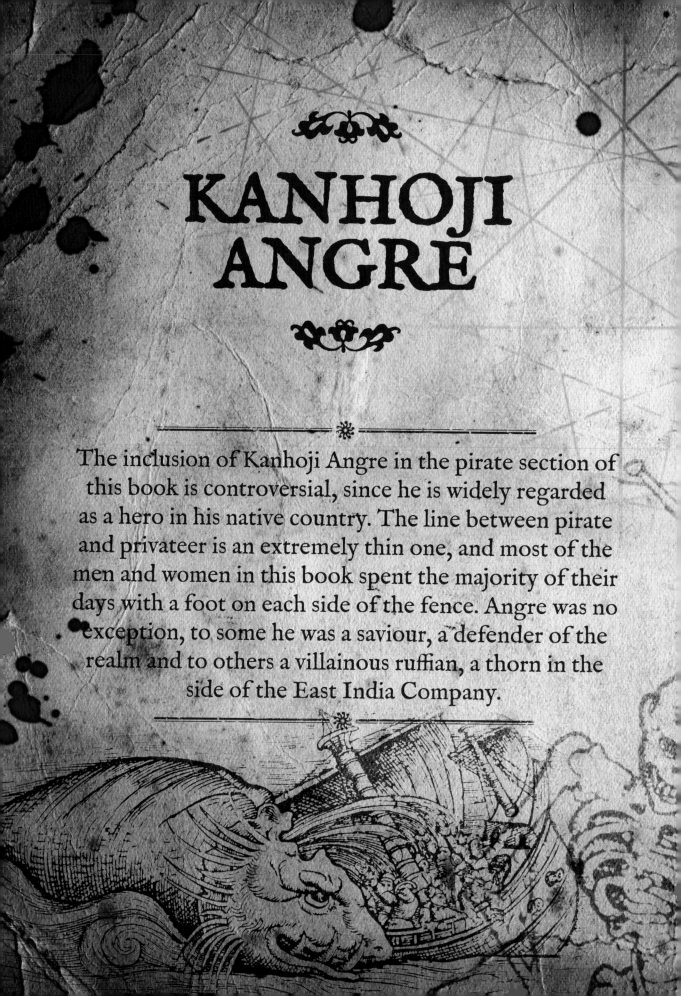

 anhoji Angre, or Angria, as he is sometimes called, was an Indian Admiral who fought for his country during the 18th century, pitting his fleet against the various European powers (mainly British, Portuguese and Dutch) that were attempting to colonize the area. Because of his frequent attacks on the British navy and merchant enterprises such as the British East India Company, he became known in Europe as a pirate. By contrast, in India he was celebrated as a heroic freedom fighter, since throughout his life he put up a spirited defence of his country, inflicting a great deal of damage on colonial interests, and by the time he died in 1729, had remained undefeated in battle.

## BRILLIANT STRATEGIST

Kanhoji was born in the coastal town of Alibag in the Konkan region of Maharashtra, India, now a popular seaside resort for residents of Mumbai. His people were among the Angri tibes of Northern Konkan, and his father, Tanoji Angre, was a high-ranking military man in the service of the Emperor Shivaji, who presided over the expansion of the Maratha empire. As a child, Kanhoji spent time at the great shipbuilding centre of Fort Suvarnadurg, where he watched the ships for the Maratha Navy being assembled. As a young man, Kanhoji joined the Maratha Navy, at a time when the Maratha empire was at its height, spanning most of India. Kanhoji's brilliance as a naval strategist meant that he soon rose to become the protector of most of the Western coast of India, from Mumbai to present-day Vengurla. In this capacity, he began to attack merchant ships of the British East India Company. The company traded in such commodities as tea, silk, cotton, indigo dye, saltpetre and opium, but it was not simply a commercial enterprise; it was backed by the British crown and had great military and administrative power in India, to the detriment of the indigenous peoples there.

## A COMMON PIRATE?

Conscious of the British threat to the Maratha empire's power, Kanhoji began to attack the East India Company's ships on a regular basis. As a result, he soon made a name for himself among the upper echelons of Indian society, including the emperor, and was promoted to the position of Admiral of the entire Maratha Navy. Among the British, however, he continued to be seen as a common pirate.

Kanhoji marked the beginning of his reign of independence by capturing a ship and its English crew near Cochin – now called Kochi, a town on the south-west coast. He followed this up by defeating the Siddi, a black African people, who were descendents of slaves and who had established settlements on the Western island of Janjira. In 1710, after fighting against the British ship the *Godolphin*, in a battle that lasted two days, Kanhoji went on to capture two islands near Mumbai, the Kanderi and Underi. He fortified them both to use as a base, and from here, he monitored all shipping coming in and out of the port, levying a tax on the British merchant vessels using the harbour. The British were infuriated, but there was nothing that they could do to stop Kanhoji – for the time being.

## MURDER AND BLACKMAIL

Little by little, Kanhoji's power increased, until he had created an autonomous zone of his own, establishing more bases in islands off the coast, such as the Andaman Islands, making attacks on British, Dutch and Portuguese shipping as he thought fit, and even issuing his own currency. With the might of the Marathan Navy at his disposal, consisting of hundreds of warships, and the support of the Indian Emperor, Kanhoji was able to rule the coast for many years, much to the chagrin of the British East India Company and the British Navy.

In 1712, Kanhoji captured a British armed yacht belonging to the British President of Mumbai, William Aislabie, and killed the head of one of his factories, Thomas Chown. He later ransomed the yacht, along with Chown's wife, who had been taken prisoner, demanding a huge sum of 30,000 rupees. On 13 February 1713, the ransom was paid and the woman released. Afterwards, Aislabie was forced to sign a treaty with Kanhoji, promising him that he would stop harassing his bases.

## STORMING THE FORT

Four years later, Mr Aislabie was replaced by a new governor – Charles Boone. Under orders to curb the power of Kanhoji, who by now had become the scourge of the colonial authorities in India, Boone commanded the British Navy to attack Kanhoji's fortifications. However, Kanhoji and his men managed to repel the attacks, even

though the forces ranged against them were considerable. In 1718, Kanhoji captured three of the British ships, blockaded the port of Mumbai, and demanded another ransom, this time from the East India Company. Once again, the British were forced to pay up, and had to concede defeat.

However, the British continued to pit their, often superior, forces against Kanhoji, whom they considered to be no more than an impudent adventurer. In 1720, they launched a further campaign, attempting to storm Kanhoji's fort at Vijaydurg, a harbour on India's West Coast. The attack was unsuccessful and the British were forced to retreat back to Mumbai. The following year, a further attack was made on the coastal town of Alibag, held by Kanhoji. This time, the British joined forces with the Portuguese, but to no avail. Kanhoji's men fought off the attack, and once again, the episode ended in failure for the colonial forces.

## THE LEGACY

By the end of his life, Kanhoji had reached a position where he controlled the entire western coastline of India. On 4 June 1729, he died, leaving his five sons to continue his reign. Since three of the sons were illegitimate, there was a certain amount of disagreement over who should rule, but eventually the territory was split between two of them. However, over the ensuing years, the Angre regime began to crumble, until it was finally destroyed with the imprisonment of Kanhoji's son Toolaji, in 1755.

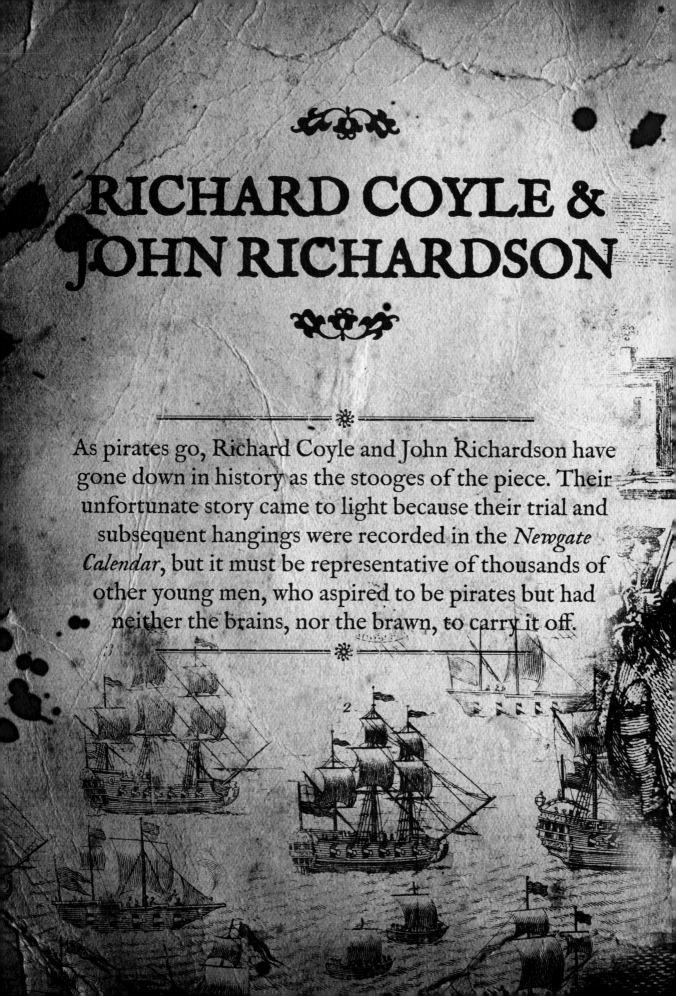

# RICHARD COYLE & JOHN RICHARDSON

As pirates go, Richard Coyle and John Richardson have gone down in history as the stooges of the piece. Their unfortunate story came to light because their trial and subsequent hangings were recorded in the *Newgate Calendar*, but it must be representative of thousands of other young men, who aspired to be pirates but had neither the brains, nor the brawn, to carry it off.

The criminal world has always attracted its fair share of blunderers and idiots, and the world of piracy is no exception. In the 17th century, during the period sometimes called 'the golden age of piracy' – although the reality was a good deal more sordid and violent than the name would suggest – the high seas became a haven for thieves, vagabonds and ne'er-do-wells from all over the world. Richard Coyle and John Richardson fell into this category, two incompetent thugs who murdered their captain while at sea, turned pirate, and were caught before they could make a single attack on an enemy vessel.

## CONFIDENCE TRICKSTER

The *Newgate Calendar*, a record of all those tried at Newgate Prison in London, gives a lurid and somewhat salacious account of John Richardson's life up until the time of the captain's murder. He was apparently born in New York, went to school, and was then apprenticed as a cooper, or barrel-maker, which was his brother's trade. However, young John evidently found the trade dull, and sailed off on a merchant ship, before coming home to work as a carpenter. All went well for five years, but he then seduced his master's daughter, and when she became pregnant, instead of owning up, he fled, serving on a warship bound for England.

In England, he began a pattern that he was to repeat over and over again in his life. He would form an illicit relationship with a woman, usually one married to a seafaring man, and then when her husband returned, disappear, making off with the valuables in her household. At other times, he would gain the friendship of a man, only to seduce his wife. In one case, he made friends with a Mr Brown, who had three daughters and four maidservants. The writer of The *Newgate Calendar* recounts that 'Richardson made presents of India handkerchiefs to all the girls, and so far ingratiated himself into their favour that in a short time all of them were pregnant.' Needless to say, when he was found out, he immediately absconded.

Despite his behaviour, Richardson must have had considerable personal charm, because over and over again his friends and lovers forgave him, allowing him a second chance. In one instance, he seduced a woman, and then both her daughters, who each became pregnant. The woman finally persuaded him to marry one of them, which in this instance he did, only to disappear to sea the day after the wedding.

## MURDER PLOT

These escapades continued until, putting his old trade to use, Richardson took a job as a ship's carpenter, on-board the vessel of one Captain Benjamin Hartley. It was here that he met Richard Coyle, a sailor who, according to *Newgate*, had a blameless record up to that point. Coyle was from Exeter, Devon, and had been apprenticed as a sailor at a young age. He had made his way up in the seafaring world, finally becoming a captain. For 17 years, he sailed his vessel to and from the port of London. However, by the time he met Richardson, his fortunes had changed, and he had been reduced to working as a ship's mate. It may have been this disappointment that prompted him to make the biggest mistake of his life.

Together, Coyle and Richardson decided to murder their captain and turn pirate. However, it appears that they did not give much thought to the details of their plan, such as what they would do afterwards, and how they would gain the support of the rest of the crew, including three boys who were apprentices on the ship. Philip Wallis, one of the boys, later testified at the Old Bailey, giving a graphic description of what happened.

According to Wallis, when Coyle approached Hartley with an axe, Hartley begged for his life, crying out plaintively, 'Dear Mr Coyle, why are you against me?' and – seeing Richardson behind him – 'my dear Carpenter, are you against me too?' However, his pleas fell on deaf ears, and the two murderers, along with another man, a Dutchman named Larson, brutally attacked Hartley with an axe and a blunderbuss, pushing him overboard into the sea.

## NO REMORSE

Having dispensed with the captain, they ransacked his cabin, but found no money. So when they put ashore to get provisions, they had to take the captain's silver spoons and his watch to sell. Meanwhile, under cover of darkness, while the ship was at anchor, the boys stole out, rowed ashore, and raised the alarm on land. Coyle and Richardson were pursued and later arrested. They were both charged with murder.

Not surprisingly, once in the dock Coyle and Richardson told different stories, each blaming the other for the murder. However, they did not persuade the judge of their innocence. It was clear that they were lying, and there were numerous witnesses, in the shape of the cabin boys, to prove it. They were both sentenced to death.

The *Newgate Calendar* relates that after the conviction, Coyle confessed his guilt, and showed a great deal of remorse for what he had done. In letters to friends, he said that he was ready to give his life in atonement for his crime. Richardson, however, appeared not to care in the slightest: 'he seemed regardless of the dreadful fate that awaited him; and having lived a life of vice and dissipation, appeared altogether indifferent to the manner in which that life should end.'

Richard Coyle and John Richardson were hanged at Execution Dock on 25 January 1738. The *Newgate Calendar's* writer commented, rather sanctimoniously: 'With regard to Coyle, we do not hear that he had been guilty of any notorious crime but that for which he died; but the life of Richardson was such a continued scene of irregularity, deception and fraud, as is almost unequalled. His treachery to the many unhappy women of whom he pretended to be enamoured was, alone, deserving of the fate which finally fell to his lot.'

# THE PIRATE CODE

It may be surprising to learn that aboard a pirate ship there was a set of rules; a list concerned with how treasure was divided up, how the injured would be compensated and what time lights must be blown out. The crew member was asked to sign their name or make their mark, swearing allegiance to the captain, an act that formally inducted them into the crew and entitled them to vote for officers and other 'affairs of moment'. Occasionally they'd swear on a bible, but in true pirate style they were more likely to swear on a human skull, crossed pistols, swords or astride a cannon. Ironically, captured recruits, particularly valuable officers such as carpenters and ship's navigators, were often forced to sign the code – a fact that seems to contradict the democratic purpose of having a code of conduct in the first place. On other occasions willing recruits asked pirates to force them into signing, because they believed a judge may be softer on them had they been forced to turn pirate under duress. Generally men who had not signed the code had a much better chance of acquittal at trial if arrested. Many pirate codes have failed to survive because pirates on the verge of capture often burnt or threw them overboard to avoid them being used as evidence against them, but fortunately a few have survived, either in part or in their entirety.

The articles varied from captain to captain but they usually covered the same ground. Here is an example of a real code of conduct, as devised by Bartholomew Roberts, aka Black Bart, written in 1721.

## ARTICLE I

Every man shall have an equal vote in affairs of moment. He shall have an equal title to the fresh provisions or strong liquors at any time seized, and shall use them at pleasure unless a scarcity may make it necessary for the common good that a retrenchment may be voted.

## ARTICLE II

Every man shall be called fairly in turn by the list on-board of prizes, because over and above their proper share, they are allowed a shift of clothes. But if they defraud the company to the value of even one dollar in plate, jewels or money, they shall be marooned. If any man rob another he shall have his nose and ears slit, and be put ashore where he shall be sure to encounter hardships.

## ARTICLE III

None shall game for money either with dice or cards.

## ARTICLE IV

The lights and candles should be put out at eight at night, and if any of the crew desire to drink after that hour they shall sit upon the open deck without lights.

## ARTICLE V

Each man shall keep his piece, cutlass and pistols at all times clean and ready for action.

## ARTICLE VI

No boy or woman to be allowed amongst them. If any man shall be found seducing any of the latter sex and carrying her to sea in disguise he shall suffer death.

## ARTICLE VII

He that shall desert the ship or his quarters in time of battle shall be punished by death or marooning.

## ARTICLE VIII

None shall strike another on-board the ship, but every man's quarrel shall be ended on shore by sword or pistol in this manner. At the word of command from the quartermaster, each man being previously placed back to back, shall turn and fire. If any man do not, the quartermaster shall knock the piece out of his hand. If both miss their aim they shall take to their cutlasses, and he that draweth first blood shall be declared the victor.

## ARTICLE IX

No man shall talk of breaking up their way of living till each has a share of 1,000. Every man who shall become a cripple or lose a limb in the service shall have 800 pieces of eight from the common stock and for lesser hurts proportionately.

## ARTICLE X

The captain and the quartermaster shall each receive two shares of a prize, the master gunner and boatswain, one and one half shares, all other officers one and one quarter, and private gentlemen of fortune one share each.

## ARTICLE XI

The musicians shall have rest on the Sabbath Day only by right. On all other days by favour only.

# PIRATE PUNISHMENTS

Punishments aboard a pirate ship were harsh. It would be quick to toss a crew member overboard for his crimes, but more inventive penalties were sometimes employed. Crimes committed on-board could range from stealing treasure from the ship's booty to inter-pirate relations of the sexual kind, but the crimes that incurred the most severe punishments were sedition or mutiny.

## DUNKING FROM THE YARDARM

The offender is securely fastened to a spar, which is hoisted high above the ocean, and repeatedly dunked into the water as many times as deemed necessary. This process also formed part of a traditional ceremony when crossing the equator.

## FLOGGING WITH A CAT O' NINE TAILS

This saw the offender being whipped with a multi-tailed implement. The number of lashes administered depended on the severity of the offence. In extreme cases the offender would be rowed round a port in an open boat and would receive lashes, this was known as 'flogging around the fleet'. Each ship in the port either took part in the whipping or merely witnessed it, the punishment serving as a reminder of what awaited those guilty of insubordination. According to legend Charlotte De Berry's first husband, Jack Jib was flogged around the fleet.

## HANGING

This was the fate that awaited most pirates and many regarded it as little more than an occupational hazard. Sometimes a pirate was hanged by his own kind, and in this case the offender would be hung from somewhere highly visible like the yardarm. Once dead, the corpse would remain there for some time as a warning to the rest of the crew. Hanging was also the main state-sanctioned punishment for piracy, so even if a pirate managed to avoid being hung by his own brethren, he could well expect the same punishment if he was ever arrested and charged.

During the golden age of piracy, hangings were spectacular public events designed to warn the population about the evils of sea robbery, and they often involved much pomp and ceremony. The actual method of hanging was very simple though. The guilty offender stood on the back of a horses cart and a cloth was placed over his head, then after the final farewells had been said, the executioner gave the call and the horse pulled away quickly, leaving the pirate dangling by his neck, where he slowly choked to death.

RIGHT: Captain Kidd hanging in irons.

An alternative method was sometimes employed to give the crowd a better view. This involved the construction of a higher crossbeam and pulley system over which the noose was slung. The noose went over the pirate's neck and the other end was connected to a horse. When the executioner gave the signal the horse bolted and the pirate was lurched high into the air, so all around could see him dance the devil's jig.

## HANGING IN IRONS

This punishment was usually reserved for notorious pirates, such as Captain Kidd, who was executed in 1701 and John Gow, who was hung in irons in 1725. The hanging took place as normal, albeit in front of a larger-than-average crowd. However instead of being buried in an unmarked grave, the body was subjected to a secondary punishment designed to drive the authorities' point home still further. First the corpse was taken away and dipped in tar to preserve it from the elements, then it was fitted in a specially made harness of iron hoops and chains to keep the body upright and, last but not least, hung up in a prominent place – usually at a port entrance or a place where potential pirates would pass by, where it could be gawked at by passing thrill-seekers, slowly rotting until nothing much remained. Obviously, the pirate in question had no sense of what was happening at this point, but during this period many believed that the soul of an unburied person would not pass into the afterlife but remain in the mortal realm, unpardoned by God for eternity. For a religious man this was the worst of all punishments.

## KEELHAULING

This was a particularly nasty form of punishment used, not by Blackbeard or Bartholomew Roberts, but by the Royal Navy. The chain of command on-board a naval vessel differed significantly from that of a pirate ship in that, in the navy, the captain was the law and could dish out any punishment he saw fit. As a result many of the punishments meted out were exceptionally cruel, and intended more as a death sentence than a slap on the wrist, as is the case with keelhauling.

Keelhauling entailed stripping the sailor naked, binding his arms and legs and tying him to a rope, which was then passed underneath the ship from port to starboard, taking the sailor with it. It was then up to members of the crew to pull the man back out of the water, across the bottom of the boat. If the man was pulled up quickly his body would most likely scrape against barnacles attached to the ship and he would suffer horrendous lacerations across his body. If he was pulled up slowly, he was likely to drown in the process. There was a risk that the rope would snap whilst rubbing against the keel, whereby the sailor would stay trapped beneath the ship, and there was also a chance that, if the offender survived, the captain would be unsatisfied and order the punishment a second time.

## MAROONING

This meant deserting the offender on an island without fresh water. Marooning was a common punishment for sodomy, and if that had been the offence, the pair would be left on the island together. Sometimes they would be left with a knife or loaded pistol so they could commit suicide if so desired.

## SLAVERY

Disobedient pirates would be sold into slavery, this was an especially popular form of retribution because it was both a punishment and a money-making exercise, killing two birds with one stone.

## TYING TO THE MAST

This was fairly straightforward, the offender was tied to the ship's mast and remained there for

days, even weeks, at the captain's discretion. In one particular case, a cabin boy who was caught stealing rum from the captain's quarters was whipped, pickled in brine and tied to the mast with his arms and legs extended to full length for nine days and nights. At the end of his ordeal, the sadistic captain was still not satisfied, so he had the unfortunate cabin boy untied and laid across the gangway, insisting that the crew walk over him in the course of their duties. They refused, and the captain was hanged.

## Walking the plank

This is probably the punishment most often associated with piracy, but there is little evidence to suggest it was practised as often as is popularly thought. The offender was blindfolded and sometimes weighed down, their hands were tied behind their back and they were then made to walk the plank until they fell into the water and drowned. In warmer waters sharks were known to follow ships, ready to feed on any tasty pirate bits and pieces they might be lucky enough to come across, so a prisoner who was forced to walk the plank could well expect to

end up being eaten by one. Walking the plank was usually a punishment chosen by squeamish pirates and those who preferred to think they had not been directly responsible for another man's death. Obviously, forcing someone to plunge into shark-infested waters is as much murder as any other form of killing, but it avoided actual bloodshed and therefore enabled some to sleep better in their beds.

## Woolding

This is a term meaning to wrap, or wind. It pertains to a punishment that involved winding a piece of rope around a pirate's eyes and slowly tightening it until the victim's eyeballs popped out of their sockets.

# Privateers

# THE BARBAROSSA BROTHERS

The Barbarossa brothers came to dominate the Barbary Coast during the late 15th century. Named after the eldest brother's infamous blood-red beard, they made their fortune defending the Ottoman Empire from the Knights of St John, who were nowhere near as saintly as their name suggests.

The Barbarossa brothers were pirates known as 'corsairs' who operated off the coast of North Africa. From the 15th to the 18th century, the corsairs were a threat to shipping of all kinds. They built Muslim fortresses in the ports of Algiers, Tripoli and Tunis, along what was, at that time, known as the Barbary coast, and made their raids with the tacit approval of the sultan of Tunisia, who received a share of the booty in return for allowing them to use Tunis as their headquarters. The most famous of the Barbary corsairs, as these Muslim pirates became known, were Aruj Barbarossa (also called Oruc or Aroudj) and his brother Khayreddin (also known as Heyreddin or Hizir).

## THE RED-HAIRED PIRATE

Aruj and Khayreddin were born on the island of Lesbos, to Yaqub, a soldier, and his wife, Katerina. Yaqub was a member of the Janissaries, the private troops who worked for the Ottoman sultan as household protectors and bodyguards. The boys' mother, Katerina, was the widow of a former Christian priest. She went on to have a total of six children with Yaqub, Aruj was the eldest and Khayreddin the youngest. There were two other sons, Ishak and Ilyas, and two daughters. The exact dates of the children's births are not known, but they appear to have been born during the 1470s.

As well as working as a soldier for the Sultan, Yaqub was also an artisan, making pots and selling them by boat around the islands. His sons helped him in his business, until they grew old enough to make a living of their own. Aruj was noticeable because of his red hair and beard, and he soon earned the nickname 'Barbarossa' – Redbeard – a name that also came to be used for his brother Khayreddin, although Khayreddin was dark-haired.

## THE KNIGHTS OF ST JOHN

With their knowledge of the sea, the brothers began their adult lives as sailors, plying the waters of the Mediterranean as traders in various commercial enterprises. They then bought their own boats and began to make a living as privateers, emerging as a sizeable force against the Knights of St John, a Christian order that ruled the island of Rhodes during this period. Despite their pious religious doctrines, the Knights were actually pirates, attacking Ottoman ships on a regular basis and inflicting a great deal of damage on the merchant shipping of the Ottoman empire. The Barbarossa Brothers, as they became known, acted as a counterbalance to the Knights, protecting the Muslim ships from attacks by the Christians. Aruj in particular became famous as a leading opponent of the Knights, and was known as an educated man who spoke several languages including Arabic, Greek, Italian, Spanish and French.

It was not long before the Knights and the Barbarossa Brothers crossed swords, since both factions were trying to control the same area of the Mediterranean. On a trip back from Tripoli, Lebanon, where he had been trading goods, Aruj's ship was captured by the Knights. Aruj was wounded and his brother Ilyas killed. Aruj was taken prisoner and remained at Bodrum Castle, now in Turkey, for three years until his brother Khayreddin came to his rescue and helped him to escape.

## BOMBING RAIDS

Not surprisingly, when Aruj came out of jail, he had a strong antipathy towards the Knights, and began to redouble his efforts against them. He was supported by Prince Shehzade Korkud, who made him an admiral in the Ottoman navy and gave him a fleet of 24 ships. As part of the Ottoman fleet, Aruj made bombing raids on Christian bases around Italy. When Shehzade was ousted in a dynastic dispute, he managed to continue a successful career working for the Mamluks, a powerful military caste who had seized power in Egypt. Aruj continued to hound the Christian crusaders, backed by an ever-changing array of Muslim potentates, until he and his brothers became one of the richest families in the Mediterranean.

## THE BARBARY CORSAIRS

In 1512, while fighting against the Spanish, Aruj sustained a serious wound in his left arm from a cannon. He was rushed to Tunis for urgent medical attention, and managed to survive the injury. However, in 1518, he was finally killed in battle, while trying to escape a siege in the town of Tlemcen, north-western Algeria. His younger brother Khayreddin took over as head of the family, and went on to become the ruler of Algiers, backed by the Ottomans.

Under Khayreddin's regime, the Spanish were expelled from Algiers, and the city became the base for all the corsairs of the region, a situation which persisted long after his death in 1547. Successive European powers attempted to quell the Barbary corsairs, but they remained in control of the region for centuries, until the French finally captured Algiers in 1830.

# SIR JOHN HAWKINS

Slave-trading pioneer; treasure-hunting pirate; high-ranking naval commander; spy; war hero — Sir John Hawkins was many things to many people. Over 400 years later, his descendants are still apologizing for the part he played in a major crime against humanity — the transporting of slaves from Africa to the Americas.

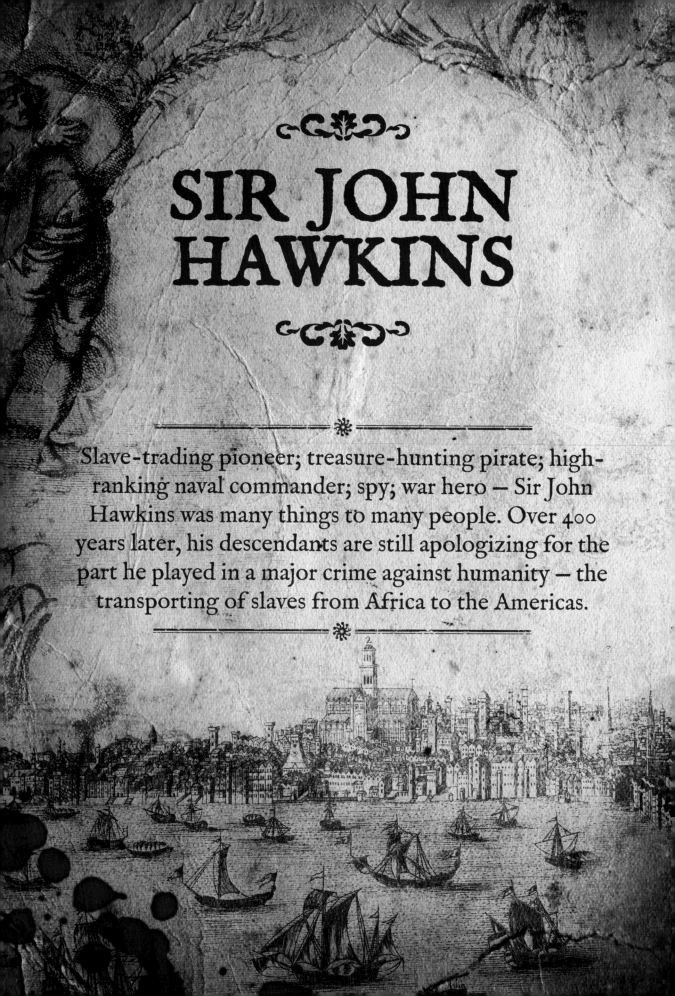

he career of Sir John Hawkins illustrates just how closely the expansion of the British empire was connected with violent crime, not only on the high seas but on land. Sir John has the dubious distinction of being the man who pioneered the British slave trade: with the blessing – and financial backing – of Queen Elizabeth I.

Sir John made a number of voyages to Africa to capture slaves, also hijacking foreign slave ships on the way. He then brought the first slaves over from Africa to work in the Caribbean, making himself and the monarchy a handsome profit in the process. Moreover, throughout his long and eventful career, Sir John continued to work as a privateer, targeting mostly Spanish treasure ships, and encouraging other pirates to do the same.

Yet despite this career of lawlessness, Sir John Hawkins became one of the most highly respected seafaring figures of his day. He was an admiral in the Royal Navy, and was knighted for his role in repelling the Spanish Armada. He was also known as an innovator, vastly improving the design of ships in the British naval fleet, and introducing better rates of pay for sailors, which resulted in a much more well-organized force. In addition, he imported a number of new commodities to Britain, including potatoes and tobacco. Few men have had such an impact on history – largely negative, but in some ways positive – as this 16th century adventurer, who appears to have straddled the roles of slave-trading privateer, treasure-hunting pirate, high-ranking naval commander, innovative shipbuilder, reforming administrator and courageous explorer with ease.

## IN SEARCH OF SLAVES

John Hawkins was born in Plymouth in 1532, the son of a merchant named William Trelawney and his wife Joan. He was the second cousin of Sir Francis Drake, with whom he was to join forces later in life, when the two fought side by side in the Spanish Armada. Following his father's footsteps, as a young man Hawkins became a merchant, and soon found a new commodity to import to Europe and the Americas: slaves.

In 1562, Hawkins gathered together a group of investors, assembled a small fleet of ships and made his first voyage to Sierra Leone. On the way, he attacked and overwhelmed a Portuguese slave ship, capturing over 300 slaves. He then travelled on to the African coast, where he captured more slaves, with the help of local slave traders there. Finding a market for them in the Caribbean, he began to ply the trade route across the Atlantic that would become central to one of history's most appalling crimes against humanity: the wholesale transporting of slaves from Africa to the West Indies and Americas, involving brutality, starvation, disease, death, exploitation and the ultimate decimation and subjugation of generations of African people.

## Vast profits

Returning to Britain, Hawkins was received with honour, having made a massive profit for his investors, and for his next voyage in 1564, he received royal patronage from Queen Elizabeth I. She helped him to pay for a very large ship, the *Jesus of Lubeck*, which was accompanied by three smaller vessels. This time, he captured around 400 Africans, transported them across the Atlantic, and sold them as slaves in what is now Colombia. He then set sail for Britain, arriving back two years later. Once again, he was received warmly, having made another vast profit for his investors.

## Spanish attack

Hawkins' next voyage, however, was not so successful. He captured around 400 slaves, some of them from Africa and some from a Portuguese slave ship, the *Madre de Deus*. His passage across the Atlantic was successful, but just as he was entering the waters of what is now Vera Cruz, Mexico, he was attacked by a Spanish fleet. All but two of his ships were destroyed, and he was forced to turn tail and head for home.

Once home, Sir John decided to stay put for a while and became a spy, helping to uncover a Spanish plot to invade Britain, for which he was rewarded with a political post as a Member of Parliament. His wife, Katherine Godson, whom he had married in 1567, had connections in high places as a result of her father Benjamin's job as treasurer of the Royal Navy. When his father-

in-law died, Hawkins took over the post and began to make many reforms in the navy. Such was the opposition from outraged traditionalists that he was taken to court on trumped-up charges of corruption, but the commission set up to investigate the charges cleared him, finding that on the contrary, the Royal Navy had improved considerably since he had taken over.

## TRIUMPH AND DISASTER

Hawkins' innovations included reforming pay and conditions for sailors, which produced a more obedient and skilful force. He also pioneered new shipbuilding methods, including caulking the underside of ships so that they were more resistant to rot and worms, and making changes to rigging so that the ships sailed faster. These improvements were to prove crucial in 1588, when the Royal Navy was pitted against the Spanish Armada. Hawkins took part in the battle as Rear Admiral, fighting alongside Francis Drake and Martin Frobisher. As is well known, the Royal Navy were victorious, and Hawkins was knighted, as were Sir Francis and Sir Martin.

In 1589, Hawkins sailed with Drake on a large armed mission to capture the Spanish treasure fleet, but this venture was unsuccessful. He then involved

himself in charity work, setting up a hospital. His final voyage, in 1595, was a treasure-hunting expedition to the Caribbean, again with Sir Francis Drake, but this ended in disaster when both of them became ill with dysentery, and died off the coast of Puerto Rico.

## Final legacy

Sir John wrote an account of his third voyage to Africa, which is entitled *An Alliance to Raid for Slaves*. This gave an explanation of the slave trade at the period, describing how the raids took place with the help and support of African merchants who were willing to sell their countrymen and women for profit, a situation which still exists to this day in many African countries. There seems to have been little understanding on his part that the slaves were human beings and should be treated as such; instead, they were captured like animals and shipped abroad to labour without pay in the plantations of the Caribbean, in a sickening trade that lasted for hundreds of years, until the abolition of slavery in the 19th century.

Thus, despite his many positive innovations, Sir John is remembered for a negative one: the pioneering of the British slave trade. In 2006, Sir John Hawkins' descendant Andrew Hawkins gave a public apology for his ancestor's behaviour, travelling to Sierra Leone to speak in front of a crowd of 25,000. When asked whether it was worth saying sorry for crimes that took place over 400 years ago, he replied simply, 'Yes. It's never too late to say sorry.' However, as some commentators have pointed out, Europeans like Sir John Hawkins were not solely to blame for the slave trade: it was rife in Africa well before he began to participate in it, and today, continues to be a shameful reality in many African countries.

# SIR MARTIN FROBISHER

---

Sir Martin Frobisher was a very successful privateer, one of the chief commanders of the Royal Navy and a favourite of Queen Elizabeth I. But all that glitters is not gold, and his life appears to have been dogged by setbacks and misfortune.

---

ike Sir Walter Raleigh and Sir Francis Drake, Sir Martin Frobisher was one of the great seafaring men of his day, and was recognized as such by Queen Elizabeth I, who commissioned many of his voyages and eventually knighted him. However, he never gained the prominence that Drake did, a fact that caused him much anguish. This was because his three major expeditions to find a north-west sea passage ended in failure. Moreover, his attempts to bring back gold ore to the queen also failed.

Frobisher spent a great deal of time and effort exporting tons of what he believed to be gold ore, only to find out that the 'black rock' he had carefully dug and transported from Canada was completely worthless. In addition, he did not find the north-west passage, although he did discover parts of Canada. For this reason, his name is not as well known as that of Raleigh and Drake today, despite the fact that he was actually a very successful privateer, capturing a number of treasure-laden ships, and that he also distinguished himself as one of the chief commanders of the Royal Navy, which defeated the Spanish Armada in 1588.

## TREACHEROUS PASSAGE

Martin Frobisher was born between 1535 and 1539 – the historical record is not accurate in this matter – in Wakefield, Yorkshire. He was the fourth son of Sir Bernard Frobisher, a Yorkshire merchant. When he was old enough to go to school, his father sent him to the home of his uncle, Sir John York, in London. Sir John was a well-known London merchant who traded overseas, so while staying in the house, young Martin was used to socializing with seafaring people. He soon began to show an interest in the maritime world, and in visiting foreign climes, so it was no surprise when, as a young man, he took up a career at sea.

Frobisher made his first voyage on a trade ship to Guinea. He then made several visits to parts of the African coast, before being commissioned, as an eminent Protestant mariner, to fight against the Spanish Catholics. But he had no intention of continuing his career as a fighting naval officer; he was more interested in exploring the world, and early on, conceived a plan to find a north-west Passage connecting the Atlantic and Pacific, along the northern coast of North America, through the treacherous waterways of the Canadian Arctic Archipelago. Opening up such a route to shipping would bring immense opportunities for trade, as goods could be exported to and from India and China (at that time called Cathay). However, it was not easy to find the money for such a venture, and for many years Frobisher was forced to fund-raise, finally finding enough support from city financiers to make his first voyage, in 1576.

## 'META INCOGNITA'

The voyage met with many setbacks. The weather was against the explorers, and when they reached Baffin Island, several of his men were taken captive by the local Inuits. Frobisher returned home, bearing with him a piece of black stone which he optimistically thought carried gold ore. Once in London, he managed to persuade the financiers to back another voyage, this time with three ships. He also received money from the queen, and the right to take possession of the lands that he found, which he duly did. (Today, Frobisher Bay is named after him.) This time, he came back with around 200 tons of the ore. Queen Elizabeth I was delighted with his claiming of new lands for the crown, which she named 'Meta Incognita', and rewarded him with a lavish reception, throwing a gold chain around his neck. Another voyage was planned, this time to continue the search for the north-west passage. However, the voyage was beset with bad luck, and the fleet of ships got lost, sailing down the Hudson River by mistake. More ore was extracted and shipped, and Frobisher's party returned to England. When the ore was more carefully examined, it was found to be worthless, and ended up being used in road construction.

## QUEST FOR GOLD

But Frobisher's career was far from over. In 1585, he became Sir Francis Drake's right-hand man, commanding an expedition to the West Indies. He was then chosen by the lord high admiral to help lead the fight against the Spanish Armada, being, as the Admiral remarked, one of four men 'of the greatest experience that this realm hath'. Along with Drake and others, he helped to repel the Spanish Armada, emerging from the fray triumphant. The queen knighted him, and from

then on he had carte blanche to operate as a privateer, which he did with great gusto, making trips to the Azores and capturing a number of French and Spanish ships. During this time, he operated both independently and in the employ of the queen. In 1594, he was sent to Brest to aid the Huguenots, or French Calvinists, in their fight against the Catholics. At Crozon, he was wounded in the fighting, and was taken back to Plymouth, where he died several days later.

Sir Martin Frobisher's career as an explorer was overshadowed by his failure to find the north-west passage. As an adventurer, he also met with failure, since his obsession with finding gold to bring back to the queen resulted in carting tons of worthless black rock over the ocean in the belief that it was precious ore. However, as a fighter, Frobisher was a great success, being knighted by the queen after helping to defeat the Spanish Armada. In addition, his career as a privateer flourished, since he captured several valuable treasure ships, but like Sir Walter Raleigh, he was not content simply to make a living as a privateer, robbing enemy ships. He had set his sights higher, as an explorer and discoverer of a fabled 'land of gold', a quest that was to dominate his endeavours and prove, in the end, to be an impossible dream.

ABOVE: This 16th century engraving celebrates the English defeat of the Spanish Armada.

# SIR FRANCIS DRAKE

Sir Francis Drake is usually remembered as a hero, the darling of Queen Elizabeth I's court, but the Spanish despised him as 'El Draque', the bloodthirsty pirate who tortured and murdered their countrymen to the extent that his behaviour helped spark a war between England and Spain.

Today, Sir Francis Drake is best remembered as the first Englishman to circumnavigate the globe, helping to discover new sea routes for shipping and to establish a more accurate map of the world. However, at the time that he lived, he was also renowned as a brilliant privateer, plundering Spanish ships and settlements in the New World to bring home treasure for the English monarchy.

As a result of his marauding exploits, he received a knighthood from Queen Elizabeth I. Not surprisingly, given his history of murder, torture and robbery against them, the Spanish hated and feared him, nicknaming him 'El Draque' (the Dragon). To them, he was far from a conquering hero, and they viewed him simply as a bloodthirsty pirate who had unlawfully attacked their countrymen. The king of Spain reputedly put a high price on his head: King Philip II was thought to have offered a reward for Drake's capture of 20,000 ducats, which today would be in the region of £4 million. Drake's raids on the Spanish possessions in the New World were certainly a factor, among others, in the eventual outbreak of war between England and Spain.

## BLOODY MARY

Francis Drake was born in Crowndale, near Tavistock, Devon, to Edmund Drake and his wife Mary Mylwaye. The family was a fairly ordinary one, his father being a farmer and preacher, and he had 11 younger brothers. Since his parents were very religious Protestants, they experienced a good deal of persecution under 'Bloody Mary', the Catholic queen of England, and had to move around the country, ending up in Chatham, Kent. At one point the family took up residence on an old ship in dry dock. This experience of being hounded by the royal authorities gave the young Francis a lifelong hatred of Catholicism, and later, he was to wreak his revenge on the Catholic country of Spain in no uncertain terms.

Whilst at Chatham, Francis began an apprenticeship aboard a small trading ship. From the age of about 13, he worked on the ship, plying routes from London across the channel to different continental ports. He remained working on the ship until he was 20, when the captain of the ship died. Drake was left the ship in the captain's will. This gave him the start he needed in life. He sold the ship, and with the proceeds, was able to mount a series of expeditions to the New World, sailing with his second cousin, Sir John Hawkins, who came from a well-known seafaring Plymouth family.

## PLUNDERING SPANISH PORTS

The first of these expeditions, in 1567, was a trading voyage to sell African slaves in the New World. However, on the way, their ships were attacked by the Spanish, resulting in the loss of many lives. The experience marked Drake for life; from that point on, he considered the Spanish to be his mortal enemy. But the failure of the voyage did not put him off adventuring. In the years to come he made many more trading expeditions to the New World, attacking Spanish settlements along the coastline there and making off with large amounts of treasure. Eventually, he became so well known for his conquests that Queen Elizabeth herself commissioned him, albeit in secret, to attack the Spanish colonizers in the New World. This he did with gusto, plundering Spanish ports along the coasts, and arriving home loaded with yet more treasure and a variety of spices and precious cloth. In one instance, he captured a Spanish ship off the coast of Peru that was loaded with around £7 million worth of gold; in another, he chased and overwhelmed a galleon full of gold, precious jewels and chests full of royal plate. This last triumph had particular significance because the location of the captured ship revealed that the Spanish were trading in areas that belonged to the Portuguese. When this information reached the Spanish court, King Philip II of Spain decided to invade Portugal, thus sparking a major conflict.

As well as his privateering successes, Drake also made a name for himself as an explorer. Among others, he discovered the existence of a navigable passage immediately south of Chile and north of the Isla Grande de Tierra del Fuego, linking the Pacific and Atlantic oceans. Shortly before entering the Straits, which were considered dangerous because of the narrowness of the channel and the unpredictable winds, Drake renamed his ship the *Golden Hind* (previously it had been called the *Pelican*.) He did this as a mark of respect to his patron, Sir Christopher Hatton, whose family crest showed a golden deer.

By now, Drake had become the scourge of the Spanish, but on returning from his voyages laden with treasure, Queen Elizabeth I rewarded him by knighting him aboard the *Golden Hind*. Not surprisingly, this infuriated the King of Spain further, and fanned the flames of war between the two countries.

## THE FINAL VOYAGE

More voyages followed, mainly to the West Indies and Florida, where Drake's looting and pillaging raids continued. He then turned his attention to the port of Cadiz in Spain, picking off 30 ships that were readying themselves for war in the harbour. When war between England and Spain finally broke out, Drake became a vice admiral, helping to defeat the legendary Spanish Armada.

At the end of the war, having played his part in the Spanish defeat, Drake went back to privateering. Now in his early 50s, he returned to the West Indies. However, this voyage proved to be his last; he became ill with dysentery and died

on 28 January 1596. His cousin John Hawkins also died of the same disease. Both Drake and Hawkins were buried at sea, and some ships that they had captured were sunk in their honour.

## LASTING LEGACY

During his lifetime, despite his many successful expeditions, and his renown as the first Englishman to circumnavigate the globe, Drake was not a universally loved figure. Some distrusted him because of his lowborn origins, and thought of him as a social climber. This, of course, was at a period in history when being a member of the nobility was seen as conferring special rights and privileges on the individual, and it was highly unusual for anyone outside the ranks of the aristocracy to become prominent in society.

Sir Francis Drake left no direct heirs. His two marriages, to Mary Newman, who died in 1583, and to Elizabeth Sydenham, who came from a noble family, produced no children. However, his legacy was a much more lasting one: he achieved worldwide fame as the Englishman who helped to map out the true geography of the world, proving that the Americas were not connected to a Southern continent, as had previously been believed, and that it was possible to sail around the bottom of South America.

He also left a rather less glorious legacy as 'El Draque' – the Dragon – who plundered and ravaged Spanish civilization in the New World, bringing its spoils back to the English monarch and thus ingratiating himself to her. Yet, however we may view his activities today, whether as an explorer, a privateer or an adventurer, there is no doubt that his achievements were astounding.

# SIR WALTER RALEIGH

Sir Walter Raleigh has become one of the most famous figures in British history. A firm favourite of Queen Elizabeth I, he could do little wrong under her reign, but in the court of King James it was a different story. When Raleigh returned home from his South American adventures in disgrace, having disobeyed the king and failed to find 'El Dorado', he was sent to the Tower of London and, eventually, beheaded.

One of the most famous figures in British history, Sir Walter Raleigh's status as an explorer, poet and favoured courtier to Queen Elizabeth I is common knowledge. What is less well known is that his expeditions to colonize parts of the New World seldom received royal patronage; instead, they were funded by himself and his friends, and their purpose was primarily to line his own pocket.

When he failed to establish English colonies in the Americas, several times, he was looked upon less favourably; and eventually, after Queen Elizabeth died and the incoming King James accused him of plotting against the throne, he was imprisoned at the Tower of London, where he spent many years. Finally, after a further adventure when he went in search of the fabled 'City of Gold', El Dorado, and attacked the Spanish against the wishes of the king, he was beheaded. Like many other privateers of his day, he had to walk a precarious line between pursuing his own interests – thereby improving his standing as a man of fortune and influence at court – and bending to whims of whichever monarch happened to be in power.

## Religious Persecution

Walter Raleigh was born into a wealthy Protestant family at Hayes Barton, a grand house in the village of East Budleigh, Devon, at some point between 1552 and 1554 (opinion is divided as to his exact date of birth). His father, who bore the same name, was a prominent nobleman, and his mother, Catherine Champernowne, had connections at court, being related to Queen Elizabeth I's governess, Kat Ashley. One of Ashley's main duties was to introduce suitable young gentlemen to court, so Walter automatically had a powerful entrée to court circles. Catherine had five sons in total, from two marriages: Walter's brother Carew Raleigh and his half brothers Humphrey, John and Adrian Gilbert. All five brothers were to prove important figures, but Walter became the most celebrated.

Despite their wealth and position, as a well-known Protestant family, the Raleighs were subject to religious persecution. As a child, Raleigh often witnessed his family on the run from 'Bloody Mary', the Catholic Queen Mary I. On one occasion, his father was forced to hide in a church tower to escape execution. As a result of these early experiences, the young Walter developed an abiding loathing for Catholicism, which he did little to hide when the Protestant Elizabeth I acceded the throne.

## The Jealous Queen

As a young man, after attending Oxford University, Raleigh fought on the side of the Huguenots in France before settling in London to study law. But his was not to be the quiet life of a scholar. Instead, he went to Ireland and helped to suppress various uprisings against English rule, also foiling a Catholic plot to dethrone the queen. As a result of these activities, he became a court favourite. Legend has it that, on one occasion, when the queen was forced to step out into a muddy street, Raleigh laid down his cloak for her to walk on. Whether or not this is true no one knows, but he certainly had a very close relationship with her. However, this was not always to his advantage. When he fell in love with one of her maids of honour, Bessie Throckmorton, Elizabeth was so jealous that she had him thrown into the Tower of London. Eventually, however, he was released and he married Bessie, to whom he remained devoted for the rest of his life.

LEFT: Queen Elizabeth I commissions Sir Walter Raleigh to sail to America.

## EL DORADO

Like many other English noblemen of the day, Raleigh was keen to explore the world, to colonize foreign countries, and to bring back treasures from far-off lands – all of which would, of course, increase his standing at court and ensure security for his family. He had heard stories of a 'City of Gold' – El Dorado – in South America, and in 1594, set off to find it. Legend had it that this golden land existed in the forests around the Orinoco river. However, his voyage was unsuccessful. When Queen Elizabeth died, his fortunes took a further turn for the worse, as the new Catholic king, James I suspected him of being involved in a plot to overthrow him, and imprisoned him once more in the Tower of London. He remained there for the next 12 years, with a death sentence hanging over him, but was finally released.

Hoping to find favour at court once more, Raleigh then set off on another expedition to find El Dorado. This was no more successful than the first, and indeed made him even more unpopular with the king, because on the way, Raleigh and his men sacked the settlement of San Thome, situated on the Orinoco, killing many Spaniards. Several of Raleigh's men were killed too, including his son, also named Walter. This event was to prove Raleigh's undoing. He had had strict instructions from the king not to harm any Spaniards on his travels, so when he finally returned to England – without the legendary treasure he had set out to find – King James was furious. Under pressure from the Spanish ambassador, the king announced that the death sentence would be re-invoked, and that this time Raleigh would be beheaded.

## THE ULTIMATE CRIME – FAILURE

The beheading of Sir Walter Raleigh took place on 29 October 1618. Raleigh did not want to show that he was afraid, and asked the executioner to dispatch him quickly. He asked to see the axe that would be used to kill him, commenting as he looked at it, 'this is a sharp medicine, but it is a physician for all diseases and miseries'. As he lay waiting for the axe to fall, he once again told the executioner to hurry; his final words were, 'Strike, man, strike!' According to the customs of the day, his severed head was embalmed and presented to his wife, who was said to have taken it with her wherever she went.

Although by the time he died, Raleigh was no longer a prestigious figure at court, many felt that his execution was extremely unjust. Had he been a favourite of the king's, as he had been under Elizabeth I, his quelling of the Spanish force might have been seen as brave and courageous, instead of being viewed as a crime punishable by death. In the same way, had he returned loaded with treasure from the imaginary 'City of Gold', he would probably have been given a hero's welcome. As it was, he had his head cut off, as a warning to others not to go against the king's commands.

The life, and death, of Sir Walter Raleigh is a salutary reminder that in the 16th and 17th centuries, privateering – even for a highborn nobleman – was an extremely precarious business. Those who succeeded were certain to be rewarded and held in the greatest esteem, while those who failed could easily be put to death or imprisoned. For in a world where there was virtually no law and order on the high seas, and little sense of cooperation, respect or commitment to justice among the European monarchs, the only real crime, it seems, was failure.

# SIR CHRISTOPHER NEWPORT

Sir Christopher Newport is well known for his part in creating the first English settlement in North America — Jamestown, Virginia. He was also a privateer of some note, who — when he was not introducing Virginian tobacco to European coffee houses, or claiming the islands of Bermuda for the Crown, was busy robbing enemy ships of precious stones, silks and spices.

 **S**ir Christopher Newport's claim to fame is that in 1607 he helped to found the first English settlement in North America, at Jamestown, Virginia. Two years later, he inadvertently colonized Bermuda for the British when he was shipwrecked on the reef there after encountering a hurricane. The passengers on-board included the admiral of the Virginia Company charged with colonizing the lands, Sir George Somers. Somers, like Newport, survived the wreck, and went on to claim the island, and the islands around it, for Britain.

But less well known than his part in the colonizing of North America and the West Indies, is the fact that Sir Christopher was an extremely successful privateer. Before his adventures in Virginia, he had made his name by capturing a number of Spanish and Portuguese ships, including the biggest prize of the century, the *Madre de Deus*, a galleon loaded with 500 tons of precious stones, silks and spices. It was for this reason that he came to the attention of the court.

## BABY CROCODILES

There is little information about the early life of Newport, but we know that for many years he worked as an independent privateer in the Caribbean and the Atlantic, capturing Spanish cargo ships. He was funded by a number of London merchants who purchased the treasures he stole from the ships. As well as gold, silver, jewels, silks and spices, he sometimes brought back live animals. On one occasion, he presented King James I with two baby crocodiles. Not only did this put him in the king's favour, but it was also good publicity, and soon Newport became one of the most famous privateers of his day, receiving commissions from the monarchy. It is strange to think that this adventurer, now hailed as a founding father of Jamestown, Virginia, was also engaged in robbing enemy ships and bringing the spoils back to his royal sponsors in Britain.

In 1606, Newport was hired by the Virginia Company of London, whose mission was to establish a colony in North American lands claimed by the British crown. He set sail in December of that year with three ships, including the largest, the *Susan Constant*, which he himself captained. The ships arrived at their destination months later, landing at Cape Henry and mounting an expedition inland to explore their surroundings. During the trip, the settlers held an election and also mounted a trial with a judge and jury against one John Smith, who was accused of mutiny. Smith was acquitted and this election and trial are celebrated today as the first instances of democratic activity to take place in North America.

## DISEASE, STARVATION AND DEATH

After many setbacks, Newport's little expedition chose a site on which to build their colony. Today, this is known as Jamestown Island. One of the aspects of the site that attracted them was that there appeared to be no Native Americans living there. They soon found out why. The area was a swamp, and few wild animals lived there, so hunting any kind of game was impossible. In addition the water was foul, and the air thick with mosquitos. The settlers, who consisted of English, German and Polish farmers and woodcutters, were inexperienced in managing such conditions and soon succumbed to disease, dying of fever, dysentery and malnutrition. Not only that, but the apparently uninhabited area turned out to be near an encampment of Paspahegh Indians, who attacked the settlers, killing one and wounding several more.

## THE SWEET SMELL OF SUCCESS

Nevertheless, despite these problems the settlers were determined to stay, so Newport sailed off home to bring essential supplies for the nascent colony. It was on one of these supply missions that Newport's ship encountered a hurricane, and was washed up on Bermuda, one of a group of islands known as the 'Isle of Devils' because of its treacherous barrier reef. Because of this delay, most of the colonists back in Jamestown starved to death.

However, this was not the end of the story. On Newport's final supply voyage to Jamestown, he was accompanied by a survivor of the Bermuda shipwreck, a man name John Rolfe, who brought with him some seeds for a new type of tobacco. In a turn of events that no one could have predicted, the seeds proved to be the saving of the colony: once cultivated, they yielded good crops, and proved to be a very popular export commodity. The colony was securely established at last, and the denizens of the coffee houses of Europe were introduced to the supposedly health-giving benefits of Virginia tobacco. Newport, his part in the colonization of North America over, sailed off to the Far East, where he became a privateer for the British East India Company, until his death in Java in 1617.

# SIR RICHARD HAWKINS

Sir Richard Hawkins, sole son and heir of Sir John Hawkins, was nothing if not a chip off the old block. A respected naval commander and successful privateer, he may not have had quite the same impact on society his father had, but he certainly enjoyed a long and prosperous career as a state-sponsored sea robber.

ir Richard Hawkins was the only son of Sir John Hawkins, who along with Sir Francis Drake, was one of the most prominent naval admirals, privateers and explorers of the Elizabethan era. Sir Richard followed in his father's footsteps and had a successful, if not quite so brilliant, career as a privateer and explorer, also fighting in the British naval battle against the Spanish Armada. We know a certain amount about his life first hand, since he wrote a book entitled, *The Observations Of Richard Hawkins In His Voyage Into The South Sea In The Year 1593*. This was published shortly after his death, and, amazingly, is still in print today.

## FAMILY TRADITION

Sir Richard's father, Admiral Sir John Hawkins, married twice. His first marriage was to Catherine Gonson, daughter of Benjamin Gonson, who was the treasurer of the Royal Navy. His second was to Margaret Vaughan. Richard was his son from his first marriage to Catherine Gonson, and his only heir. The young Richard grew up in a maritime environment dominated by his father's reputation as an illustrious sea dog, so it was no surprise when he too continued the family tradition as a privateer.

Richard's first important sea voyage was to Brazil, with his uncle, William Hawkins. In 1585, he made another significant journey, this time in the company of his father's second cousin, Sir Francis Drake. The venture with Drake was a privateering one, to attack Spanish settlements along the coast of Florida and on the Caribbean islands. Richard was put in charge of a galliot, a small galley ship propelled by 20 oarsmen as well as by sails, armed with cannons, and carrying over 100 crewmen. On this expedition, the privateers brought home some stragglers from Roanoke Island, off North Carolina, who had survived Sir Walter Raleigh's attempt to found a colony there.

## ATTACK ON THE SPANISH TREASURE FLEET

We next hear of Richard Hawkins in 1588, when he commanded a privateer ship, the *Swallow*, in the battle against the Spanish Armada. He and his men fought bravely in what was an extraordinary battle against the mighty Spanish ships, who called themselves the '*Armada Invencible*' – the Invincible Navy. With their superior organizational skills, the smaller English naval force managed to drive off the Spanish fleet, thus protecting England from invasion by the Spanish King Philip II.

Not surprisingly, after the battle, relations between the English and Spanish continued to be hostile, especially at sea, and two years later Richard Hawkins accompanied his father on a series of raids against the Spanish treasure fleet. These took place off the coast of Portugal, which was then in Spanish possession. King Philip II had imposed taxes on Spain's many colonies around the world, which were paid in the form of such precious items as silver, gold, gems, silk, spices and tobacco. A heavily armed treasure fleet was needed to transport these goods back to the Spanish mainland, and this naturally enough became a target for the privateers and pirates who roamed the seas in search of booty. In addition, these 'free enterprise' individuals often had the backing of Protestant European monarchs such as Queen Elizabeth I, who had plenty of reason to resent and fear the imperialism of the Catholic king of Spain.

## BLOODTHIRSTY RAIDS

Drake's raids on the Spanish treasure fleet were not successful, and the English privateers returned home empty-handed. However, Hawkins Junior was not deterred. In 1593, he fitted out a ship, the *Dainty*, and embarked on another voyage, this time of exploration. Like Walter Raleigh, Francis Drake and his father before him, Hawkins intended to sail around the world, and saw his mission as one of geographical and scientific discovery. That said, the term 'exploration' in this period seemed to be something of a euphemism, since it included all manner of rather more aggressive activities, ranging from piracy on the high seas to bloodthirsty raids on Spanish cities, towns and settlements on land.

Sailing across the Atlantic, Hawkins followed Drake's route up the Straits of Magellan and took the opportunity on the way to raid the city of Valparaiso, now in Chile. Not surprisingly, the Spanish were not pleased by this, and as the *Dainty* sailed into the Bay of Atacames, in northern Ecuador it was attacked by a fleet of six Spanish ships. A fierce battle ensued, lasting three days. Hawkins and his crew were vastly outnumbered, but they fought bravely, and Hawkins was badly wounded. Eventually, Hawkins surrendered, but only after receiving assurance that his crewmen would be safely transported back to England. As it happened, this promise was not fulfilled.

## PIRATE TURNED MEMBER OF PARLIAMENT

After conceding defeat, the Spanish imprisoned Hawkins in Peru. Three years later, he was taken to Spain and incarcerated there, first in Seville and then in Madrid. He was released in 1602, when stepmother, Margaret Vaughan, paid the authorities a ransom for his release. By this time, his father Sir John had died, and by all accounts, Margaret was none to happy too stump up the money.

On returning to England in 1603, Richard was knighted by King James I for his pains. The following year, he received a post as Member of Parliament for Plymouth and vice-admiral of Devon, his role being to defend the coast from foreign attack, and to clamp down on piracy. This was a job he was well suited for, since he himself had effectively made a long and successful career out of robbery on the high seas.

Hawkins' later years were taken up with naval activities, including serving as vice-admiral of the fleet under Sir Robert Mansell. Once again, he was brought in to deal with pirates – in this case, Algerian privateers known as the Barbary corsairs, who were terrorizing ships in the Mediterranean. His last voyage took place in 1620, at the age of 58. The voyage was not successful, and he died two years later, just as his memoirs were being published.

# SIR MICHAEL GEARE

A man of humble birth, the life, and death, of Sir Michael Geare represents something of an exception in his field. A successful privateer who relied on his own skills as a seaman, businessman and courageous fighter rather than high-profile connections in the navy and aristocracy, he eventually retired from his career as a sea dog and died of natural causes in an atmosphere of wealth and comfort. Who says that crime never pays?

**M**any of the privateers who rose to prominence in the 16th century were the sons of aristocrats or of wealthy merchants. Sir Michael Geare, however, is thought to have been from a poor background, having been brought up in the East End of London. In an age where the British monarchy encouraged free enterprise, both on land and sea, in the form of bloodthirsty raids against the Spanish, Geare was able to make his way up in the maritime world by standing out as a skilled seaman and courageous fighter. By the time he died, he had become one of the richest privateers of his day.

## SMOOTH OPERATOR

Michael Geare was born in Limehouse, in the East End of London, in 1565. Little is known about his family, but it seems likely that it was a poor one, as when he was still in his teens he was apprenticed to a mariner. He proved an able and willing pupil, and before long was setting out on voyages with some of the best-known privateers of the day, including Sir George Carey, a cousin of Queen Elizabeth I. From 1588 to 1591 he rose steadily through the ranks, and at the end of that time was made captain of his first ship, the *Little John*. This was one of a fleet of five ships financed by Sir Francis Drake and others, whose purpose was to take part in the privateering wars raging between England and Spain in the Caribbean. During the voyage, and once engaged in battle, Geare proved to be a highly competent sailor and a fearless fighter, so much so that, on the fleet's return, the fleet's commander, William Lane, commended him to the expedition's financiers in London.

Not only was Geare a courageous sailor, he was also extremely adept at amassing wealth for himself. Having often led the charge in battle, he had also helped himself wherever possible to the choicest booty on offer, and had supplemented this by making money from smuggling operations on his home territory. It seems that, as well as being a rough and ready fighter, he was also a slick business operator; indeed, he could be viewed as one of the East End's earliest gangsters.

## JUMPING SHIP

In 1592, Geare was able to buy himself a share in the *Little John*, and went into partnership with William Lane. The pair renamed the ship the *Michael and John* and set off on a series of voyages to the West Indies. Over the following three years, Lane and Geare made four successful expeditions in the ship, returning each time loaded with Spanish treasure. However, in 1595, their luck began to run out. Sailing past Havana, Cuba, they encountered a Spanish man-of-war – the most powerful type of armed ship at that time – and engaged in battle with it. At least 50 of Geare's crew were killed or drowned in the fighting, and the Spanish also reclaimed a small ship, or pinnace, that Geare had captured earlier. Geare managed to escape the battle unscathed, and returned home, making good some of his losses by capturing another Spanish ship on the way.

The following year, Geare joined a privateering expedition with, among others, the famous explorer and privateer Christopher Newport. Numerous adventures followed, until he jumped ship in Jamaica and joined forces with Sir Anthony Shirley. (Shirley, or Sherley, was a former Member

M.

of Parliament who had travelled the world and who later became known for his writings about a voyage into Persia.) Along with another prominent privateer, William Parker, Geare and Shirley set sail for Honduras. On this voyage, Geare commanded a warship by the name of *Archangel*, and captured three treasure ships. Unfortunately for him, he did not manage to bring all three prizes home. On the way, the crew of one of the captured ships sailed off in the other direction, selling the ship and its contents in Morocco.

## DAGGER AT THE DOOR

Geare continued his privateering career into the early 17th century, when he joined forces with Newport once again to make an armed raid on Santiago, Cuba. This proved unsuccessful when he and his men were driven back by cannons and a herd of stampeding cattle, loosed on them by the Spanish governor of the city. After this debacle, Geare rather sensibly decided to retire.

In 1603, after receiving a knighthood from King James I, Geare retired to a luxurious home in Stepney, East London, where he proceeded to enjoy his immense wealth until he died. To the end, he remained proud of his reputation as a freebooting privateer, and made no attempt to hide the provenance of his ill-gotten gains: he even hung a dagger outside the door of his home in Stepney to remind passers-by of his days as a salty 'sea dog', fighting in the cause of king, country and his own coffers.

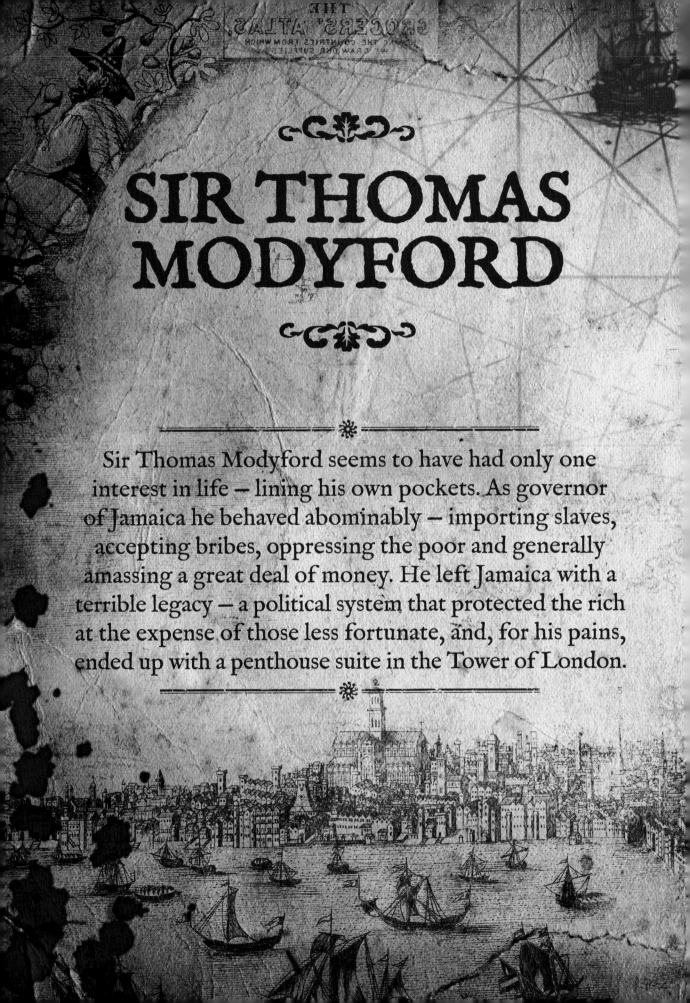

# SIR THOMAS MODYFORD

Sir Thomas Modyford seems to have had only one interest in life — lining his own pockets. As governor of Jamaica he behaved abominably — importing slaves, accepting bribes, oppressing the poor and generally amassing a great deal of money. He left Jamaica with a terrible legacy — a political system that protected the rich at the expense of those less fortunate, and, for his pains, ended up with a penthouse suite in the Tower of London.

The politicians of the island of Jamaica have a history of being corrupt and greedy. This goes back many years, to the 17th century, when Colonel Sir Thomas Modyford became the governor of Jamaica, and used his position to make a fortune out of the many pirate bands who plied the waters of the Caribbean, taking money and goods from them in exchange for pardons. Modyford is also credited with setting up the island's slave economy, since he transported thousands of slaves to Jamaica, setting up the plantations there and dividing the country into parishes so that he could oversee their operations. He worked in conjunction with a group of men called the Royal Adventurers into Africa, who traded slaves and other goods from Africa, selling them to countries in Europe and the New World. In fact, almost all the slaves that entered the West Indies came there through the auspices of the Royal Adventurers, who had a monopoly on the slave trade to the islands.

Modyford appears to have been an extremely corrupt individual, whose main aim in life was to line his own pockets. In a sense, Jamaica has been suffering the consequences of his actions ever since, with a general population whose history is scarred by slavery, cruelty and oppression, and a political system that some believe is rotten to the core, based on bribery, corruption and the self-interest of those who run the country.

## The Royal Adventurers

Thomas Modyford was an Englishman born in Exeter. His father was the mayor of the town, and the family had aristocratic connections, being related to the Duke of Albermarle. As a young man, Modyford emigrated to Barbados. Other members of his family also went with him, including his brother James. They left partly because the English Civil War had broken out, and partly because they could see that there were plenty of opportunities to make a fortune in the islands.

According to most reports, Modyford was already a rich man when he arrived on Barbados, and was able to put down an immediate deposit of £1,000 for a plantation. Over the next few years, he was able to pay the rest of the sum, amounting to £6,000 or more. He made a great deal of money by being a factor, or middle man, for the Royal Adventurers, a British company trading slaves from Africa to work in the plantations. As a consequence, his standing on the island increased, and he rose to become the Speaker of the House of Assembly.

## Convicted Felons

In the years that followed, Modyford turned his attention to the island of Jamaica. The political situation in Britain had become complicated, first with the setting up of the Commonwealth there, under Oliver Cromwell, and then with the Restoration of the Monarchy. The fact that Modyford had negotiated with both sides for his commission for a while made his position

RIGHT: The Tower of London, as seen from the River Thames, in 1647

precarious. However, he proved a skilful negotiator and on 15 February 1664, he was appointed governor of Jamaica, with a brief to set up a full-scale plantation economy there.

He arrived on the island with 700 planters and their slaves. The plantations were to be worked by unpaid African slaves. In addition, Modyford's brother James received a royal license to ship prisoners from British prisons over to the island, so that a large number of convicted felons also became part of the workforce. Thus it was that, almost overnight, Jamaica changed from being a sleepy island paradise into a brutal labour camp full of desperate slaves, overseen by corrupt, greedy politicians.

## IMPRISONED IN THE TOWER

Modyford's power increased, as did his financial interests. He lived in splendour on a cacao plantation in St Katherine's parish, at a place called Sixteen Mile Walk. There, he received the great and good from around the islands. However, before long his luck began to change. It became known that he was in league with various pirates and adventurers around the island, receiving booty from them in return for issuing them with pardons. By turning a blind eye to their activities, he was increasing the size of his coffers, but as it turned out, this was an unwise strategy. The British government were displeased that the governor was allowing law and order to be ignored on the high seas, as this discouraged trade to the islands. Therefore they removed Modyford from his post, brought him to London for trial and took him into custody. He remained in the Tower of London for two years, but in the event, the trial did not take place. Perhaps the authorities feared that other scandals might come out, ones that would not reflect well on British colonial rule in the West Indies. Whatever the case, Modyford was set free and returned to his plantation in Jamaica, where he died in 1679.

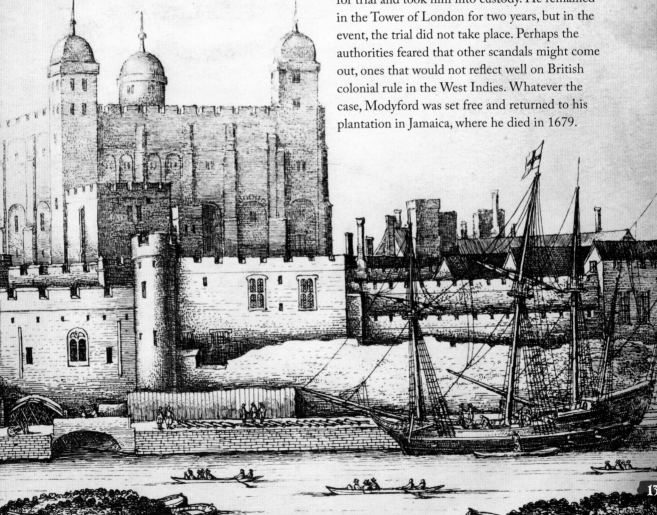

# SIR CHRISTOPHER MYNGS

Sir Christopher Myngs fell out of favour with the authorities because he had a habit of pocketing large amounts of booty instead of handing it over to the king. However, his reputation for cruelty, greed and a disagreeable personality did not stop him assembling one of the largest pirate forces in history, so he must have been doing something right.

During his lifetime Sir Christopher Myngs won the dubious accolade of assembling one of the largest pirate forces in history. In 1663, he and his wild band of buccaneers committed a series of bloodthirsty atrocities on Spanish settlements in South America, prompting the British government to forbid him from making any further attacks. Myngs also, at different times in his career, found himself out of favour with the authorities because of his habit of keeping enormous amounts of booty instead of handing it over to the king. However, despite Myngs' reputation for unnecessary cruelty, extreme greed, and a personality that the governor of Jamaica described as 'unhinged and out of tune', Myngs continued to hold high posts within the Royal Navy, such as vice-admiral, until his death from wounds sustained in battle in 1666.

## RAPE AND PILLAGE

Myngs is mentioned by Samuel Pepys as having humble family origins, but historians now dispute this. Whatever the case, he was born somewhere between 1620 and 1625 and is thought to have entered the Royal Navy as a cabin boy. We first hear of his prowess as a seaman when he captained a ship called the *Elisabeth*, fighting in the First Anglo-Dutch War. This war began by a dispute over trade, and was fought entirely at sea. Myngs distinguished himself on this occasion by capturing two Dutch man-of-war ships. After that, he was seen as a rising star in the British navy, and in 1655 was picked for the difficult job of quelling a mutiny on a warship called the *Marston Moor*. He succeeded in restoring order on the ship, and spent the following years in Jamaica, attacking Spanish treasure ships. He also made a number of raids on Spanish settlements along the coastline of South America, earning a reputation as a savage leader who encouraged his men to rape and torture the local population.

Not surprisingly, given his bloodthirsty exploits, he became enemy number one among the Spanish authorities, who saw him as a common criminal and mass murderer. They were doubly outraged by the fact that his actions appeared to be sanctioned by the British government, and demanded that the British arrest him. The British were none too pleased with Myngs either. He had not only stolen enormous amounts of booty from the Spanish settlements, but in true pirate style had shared his ill-gotten gains with his cronies instead of handing it over to the governor of Jamaica, as he should have done. Thus, the governor issued a warrant for Myngs' arrest, charging him with embezzlement, and Myngs was sent back to England in disgrace.

## MIGHTY PIRATE BAND

However, once in England, the authorities decided that Myngs was too useful an asset to the British government to be allowed to languish in jail, and sent him back to Jamaica. His brief was to continue to attack the Spanish in the Caribbean, but this time to do it in a more covert way, without drawing so much attention to himself. Myngs responded by assembling the largest fleet of buccaneers that the area had

ever seen, numbering 14 ships and over 1,000 men, including the notorious pirate Henry Morgan. This mighty band of pirates attacked San Francisco de Campeche, in modern Mexico, ransacking the town and committing dreadful atrocities. Once again, the king of England, Charles II, instructed the governor of Jamaica to forbid Myngs to make any further attacks on the Spanish. But in reality, the attacks continued, and the British turned a blind eye, since it was in their interest to undermine Spanish settlements in the area.

## VIOLENT END

After the raid on Campeche, Myngs returned to England. He had been badly wounded in the fighting and needed time to recuperate. As a reward for his bravery, he was given several posts as vice-admiral in different British fleets. Before long, he returned to battle, fighting at the Battle of Lowestoft in the Second Anglo-Dutch War. This war was another bout of hostilities between the British and the Dutch over trade. The battle, which took place at sea, was a triumph for Britain, and proved to be the worst defeat the Dutch navy had suffered in its entire history. As one of the leading commanders in the battle, Myngs covered himself in glory, and afterwards was knighted by the king. He continued to serve in the war, and in 1666 took part in another sea battle against the Dutch, known as the Four Days' Battle. This time, however, his luck ran out. He was shot in the cheek and in the shoulder, and a few days later, died of his wounds. It was a violent end to a violent life.

# FORTUNATUS WRIGHT

Like so many powerful and admired men, Fortunatus Wright was one thing in public and quite another in private. To writers and journalists of the day he was a 'brave corsair', and an 'ever victorious captain around whose name and fate clings the halo of mystery and romance'. However, in the eyes of his long-suffering father-in-law, Wright was little more than the shameless cad who seduced his daughter only to abuse and, ultimately, abandon her in order to go 'a-rambling'

ortunatus Wright was an 18th century privateer whose bold exploits in the Mediterranean earned him the title of 'the brave corsair'. He was famed as one of the most dazzling adventurers of the time, capturing a total of 16 ships with valuable cargo. The scourge of French shipping, Wright mostly operated from a base in Livorno, Italy, and was so successful that the king of France offered to give a title to anyone who could capture him, dead or alive.

We also know a little about Wright's private life from the diary of William Bulkeley, a gentleman from Anglesey, North Wales. This important historical document tells how Bulkeley's daughter Mary had the misfortune to marry Wright. Bulkeley recounts his son-in-law's cruelty to Mary, how she was cheated out of her husband's sizeable legacy after his death, how she and her children became destitute and how they all eventually returned to Wales to live with him. In fact, as a result of Wright's behaviour, Bulkeley's days became so 'troublesome', as he put it, that he eventually stopped writing about general matters altogether, and limited his diary entries to complaints about the weather – a somewhat frustrating development for contemporary historians studying the diary as a document of 18th-century life.

## BARBAROUS INSULTS

Little is known about Fortunatus Wright's childhood and early life except that he was born in Wallasey, Wirral, on 3 May 1712 to John Wright and his wife Phillipa Elworthy. As he was living near the port city of Liverpool, it is likely that he grew up learning something of seafaring life, but as a young man, he began work in the brewing and distillery trade.

Wright's first marriage to Martha Painter, also of Wallasey, produced several children, but Martha died young. We next hear of Wright from an entry in William Bulkeley's diary on 21 March

1738. Bulkeley reports that his daughter Mary has written to him 'requesting speedy consent of her being married to Fortunatus Wright forthwith … whereby she may prevent all further trouble'. The next passage in Bulkeley's diary is scratched out, but it appears that Mary had been seduced by Wright, was pregnant, and wanted to marry quickly before the baby was born. We then learn from the diary that after the marriage, Mary lost the baby, but later went on to have several more children. However, her marriage to Wright was not a happy one: Bulkeley refers to the 'barbarous usage and insults received by my daughter from her husband'. He goes on to describe the couple's quarrelling, and how Wright finally abandoned her to go 'a-rambling'.

## GREED OR PATRIOTISM?

Leaving his wife and family to fend for themselves, Wright set off to Lucca, Italy, where his first exploit was to involve himself in a fracas with the local guards there. After threatening to kill a soldier, he was imprisoned for three days before being escorted out of the city and told never to return. He then settled in the port city of Livorno in Tuscany, or Leghorn, as it was known in English. From his base there he began to involve himself in various nefarious enterprises, including privateering on behalf of the British government. At this period, during the War of the Austrian Succession, a challenge to the power of the Hapsburg monarchy involving nearly all the

European powers, meant that Britain and France were effectively at war. During the hostilities, Wright's ship the *Swallow*, was captured. In response, Wright fitted out a brigantine, the *Fame*, and proceeded to attack French shipping in the Levant, capturing and looting 16 ships.

Thus far, Wright had had the blessing of the English government for his raids. However, when he began to seize Italian and Turkish property on the French ships, the government ordered him to give back the booty. Wright refused, and was imprisoned by the Turks, who for several months refused to hand him over to the English consul. Eventually, Wright agreed to stand trial for his crimes, but by this time the war was over, and he could no longer continue his raids under the guise of patriotism. His fortunes suffered as a consequence, and he was in a very bad-tempered frame of mind when his wife Mary decided to join him in Livorno. Bulkeley reports that once again, he treated her cruelly, and the marriage continued to be as turbulent as ever.

## DROWNED AT SEA

In 1756, the Seven Years War broke out. It was a huge conflict in which over a million Europeans died, but for Wright it was a stroke of luck, enabling him to continue his privateering exploits and remove himself from his increasingly unpleasant domestic situation. He armed a ship, the *St George*, and sailed out of Livorno, once more engaging in a series of battles and skirmishes with French and other ships that flouted maritime law. After putting in at Malta to refit, Wright set sail for home, with the purpose of attacking a French man-of-war in the waters outside Livorno, but on the way the ship was caught in a huge storm. The ship was wrecked, and all the men on-board drowned, including Wright. The total loss of life was 60 men.

But that was not the end of the story. A few weeks later, a letter from a merchant in Livorno to another in Liverpool claimed that Wright was still alive, and had been seen attacking another ship on the coast of Malta. It was also suggested in the letter that Wright had later put into the port of Messina, Sicily, with the captured ship. Nevertheless these reports were never confirmed.

## THE 'HALO OF MYSTERY AND ROMANCE'

In a sad postscript to the story, it appears that Wright's wife Mary and her children were cheated out of his considerable estate by another relative. Wright's daughter by his first wife, Philippa, married a man named Charles Evelyn. When Wright died, Evelyn managed to claim his entire estate for himself and his wife, leaving Mary and her family destitute. Mary's long-suffering father Bulkeley recounts how the forlorn band came home to him: first two of his grandchildren appeared on his doorstep, followed by their mother, and then three more grandchildren. After this, Bulkeley appears to have been so downcast by the situation that he ceased to refer to it in his diary.

Today, Fortunatus Wright is remembered as one of the most flamboyant privateers of his day. The 18th-century author Tobias Smollett called him a 'brave corsair', while another writer of the day, the journalist Gomer Williams, described him, even more fancifully, 'the ideal and ever-victorious captain around whose name and fate clings the halo of mystery and romance'. But the account of him given in the diary of an ordinary Welsh gentleman, William Bulkeley, who was unlucky enough to become his father-in-law, tells a somewhat different story. Even allowing for the fact that fathers-in-law are not always the most objective of narrators, the tale of how Wright seduced the rather simple Mary, cruelly mistreated her, and then abandoned her, along with their five children, paints a decidedly less romantic picture of a man who, in his personal life, was anything but 'ideal'.

# AMBROISE LOUIS GARNERAY

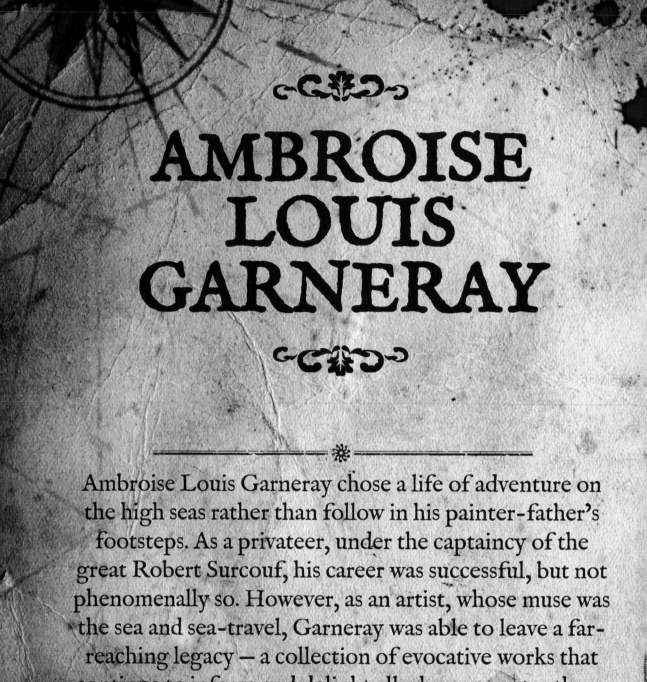

Ambroise Louis Garneray chose a life of adventure on the high seas rather than follow in his painter-father's footsteps. As a privateer, under the captaincy of the great Robert Surcouf, his career was successful, but not phenomenally so. However, as an artist, whose muse was the sea and sea-travel, Garneray was able to leave a far-reaching legacy — a collection of evocative works that continue to inform and delight all who encounter them.

orn with the smell of the salty ocean in his lungs, it is no surprise that the young Ambroise Louis Garneray craved adventure on the high seas. Born on 9 February 1783 in Paris, he was the son of a Parisian painter, Jean-François Garneray, who had been commissioned to paint for the king, Louis XVI. Although Garneray eventually followed in his father's footsteps, his first love was the sea. Driven by stories from his cousin Beaulieu-Leloup, who was commander of the frigate *Forte*, Garneray decided to join the navy in 1796 when he was just thirteen years old, going against his father's wishes.

Garneray's first commission was serving under rear-admiral Pierre César Charles de Sercey. Garneray sailed from Rochefort to the Indian Ocean with the frigate division. In fact Garneray was witness to the frigate's final destruction, when Sercey's ship, the *Preneuse*, was blown up just outside Port-Louis in Mauritius. The *Preneuse* was a 44-gun frigate which served as a commerce raider which had come under fire on many occasions, but always managing to stay out of serious trouble. Garneray took part in various campaigns under Sercey, and in 1799 was promoted to quartermaster and 'first painter of the edge' on the *Preneuse*, this time under the captaincy of Jean-Matthieu-Adrien L'hermitte. The frigate was the only remaining frigate serving in the Indian Ocean. Life was tough, rations were poor, work was gruelling and on one occasion the *Preneuse* was forced to go into quarantine because its entire crew were suffering from scurvy. Despite all the hardships Garneray loved to feel the salt water on his face and the freedom of sailing the oceans.

On 11 December 1799, when the *Preneuse* was returning to the Île de France, it was chased by the 74-gun HMS *Tremendous*, which was captained by John Osborn. As L'hermitte's ship sailed closer to the shore, her escape route was blocked by the HMS *Adamant*, under Captain William Hotham, which caused the *Preneuse* to be washed ashore by gale-force winds. The

British closed in and the *Preneuse* was heavily battered, causing the captain to instruct his crew to abandon ship. That was to be the end of Garneray's role in the French navy.

Two weeks after the destruction of the *Preneuse*, Garneray decided to pursue his career as a mariner by joining the corsair crew of the *Confiance* under Robert Surcouf. This was to be Garneray's first experience of piracy and he loved it. He loved the daring raids, the thrilling stories of looting frigates from the more experienced pirates, and his greatest thrill came when they captured the *Kent* in 1800. In March, Surcouf led a brilliant campaign which resulted in the capture of nine British ships. On 7 October 1800, in the Bay of Bengal, the *Confiance* came face to face with the 38-gun *Kent*, a 1200-ton East Indiaman with 400 crew and a company of naval riflemen. Although the crew of the *Confiance* were outnumbered three to one, the Frenchmen managed to seize control of the *Kent*. Surcouf became a living legend in France and the capture was highly valued. This was the first and only time that Garneray would make any money out of piracy.

When the *Confiance* returned to France, Garneray decided to stay in Mauritius and invest his money in a slave trading ship called *l'Union*, on which he served as first mate. His life as a pirate involved sailing on various ships trading and slaving on the African coast. After the peace

of Amiens, Garneray served on-board the *Pinson*, a cutter which was based in the Île Bourbon. When its skipper died, Garneray had a brief spell as commander of the *Pinson* before it was shipwrecked.

His next spell was on-board the corsair ship the *Tigre du Bengale*, followed by the frigate *Atalante* which was attached to the squadron of Linois. He was also on-board the *Belle Poule* when it was captured by the British in March 1806. During the capture Garneray was wounded, and he spent the remainder of the war incarcerated in the prison hulks situated off Portsmouth on-board the *Protée*, the *Couronne* and the *Vengeance* respectively. To alleviate the boredom, Garneray turned his hand to painting and even managed to make some money by selling some of his paintings to a British merchant.

## A RESPECTABLE LIVING

When Napoleon abdicated, the British freed all their prisoners. Garneray's release came on 18 May 1814, but he did not resume his career at sea. His experience during the First French Empire, by rights should have secured him a qualified position in the French Navy, but this is something that was not possible during the Restoration. Garneray returned to Paris where he became embroiled in the world of art, befriending the fashion illustrator Horace Vernet and the artist Théodore Géricault. Garneray was also introduced to the future king, Louis Philippe, who was instrumental in obtaining a commission for the ex-corsair. Garneray devoted himself to painting, following in his father's footsteps. His paintings caught the attention of Napoleon and his first official order from him was a depiction of the great man's return from Elba – the meeting of *l'Inconstant* and the *Zéphir*. He became famous for his handling of details and his rendering of dramatic atmospheric effects in landscapes.

Garneray later came under the employ of the duke of Angoulême, who at the time was grand admiral of France. He was appointed his official painter in 1817 and became the first *peintre officiel de la Marine* (official painter of the navy). In 1823, in collaboration with Étienne Jouy , Garneray painted and engraved a series of 59 coastal scenes, *Vues des Côtes de France*.

In 1833, Garneray was made director of the museum of Rouen, proving himself to be a respected citizen, despite his spell as a corsair. He is also renowned for developing a new genre of painting – the aquatint – and became famous for his superb engravings. However, despite this success, Garneray seemed to fall out of favour in the 1840s, losing nearly all of his political supporters which caused him to fall into poverty. By the time of Napoleon III's reign, Garneray went back into action and took part in the failed coup d'État of Strasbourg. At the start of the Second French Empire, the once pirate, returned to a brief spell of glory when he was awarded the Legion of Honour in 1852 by Vice Admiral Bergeret and the emperor himself.

Garneray also wrote three autobiographies which recounted his adventurous, double career as a sailor, sometimes corsair, going into graphic detail about his daring exploits alongside his fellow corsairs.

## A PITIFUL END

Shortly after receiving the award, Garneray developed a tremor which put a stop to his painting and also curbed his career as a writer. He loved to write epic tales of his adventures as a pirate, becoming one of the precursors of the maritime novel of adventure. Garneray died in 1857 just a few months after his wife was mysteriously assassinated. Garneray is buried in a cemetery at Montmartre.

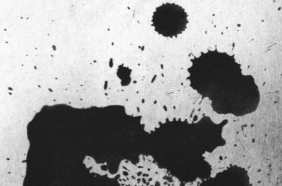

# ROBERT SURCOUF

A life-long rebel who was considered brave even
by his enemies, Robert Surcouf earned the title
'King of the Corsairs', and was decorated as a hero by
Napoleon himself. Unlike most men involved in sea
crime, Surcouf's industrious life appears to have been a
happy one. In any case, he avoided the gibbet, and his
passing was marked by a grand funeral cortege of 50
boats, illustrating just how popular a figure
this privateer had become.

**R**obert Surcouf was one of the most successful privateers, or corsairs, of his time. His fame in his native France and throughout Europe was such that he was known as 'Le Roi des Corsaires', or 'The King of the Corsairs'.

## PLAYING HOOKY

Born in December 1773, the young Robert grew up in the seaside town of St Malo, Brittany, which had been a fortified island in the Middle Ages and by the 18th century had become a well-known haunt for pirates from around the globe. He attended a Jesuit school, but his strict religious education did not prevent him from hankering after a seafaring life. Legend has it that at the age of just 13, he slipped away from school, stole a boat and went sailing on the sea. However, he encountered a storm and was lucky to be rescued by the coastguard, who brought the truant home. Undeterred by this failure, Robert continued to dream of a life on the ocean wave, and when he left school, he found work on a merchant ship travelling to India. He was only 15 years old when he made this first voyage.

## WAR HERO

On Surcouf's return to France several years later, he found there had been radical changes, as a result of the French Revolution. The new regime favoured independent entrepreneurs like himself, and he soon took advantage of the situation. Sailing to Mauritius, which at the time was a French colony named Ile de France, he became involved in hostilities against the British, who were trying to take control of the island. As second in command of the warship *Cybele*, Surcouf helped to repel the British navy, in a battle that went down in history as a triumph for the French. This was because Surcouf had a far smaller fleet than the British, yet still managed to win the day.

In the years that followed, Surcouf continued to be a thorn in the side of the British. In 1794, on a voyage to Mauritius, he captured three

British ships by means of trickery. As he sailed by, he failed to raise the French flag, whereupon the British ships fired a warning shot. He took the warning shot as meaning that the British wanted to engage in battle, and promptly began to fire back in self-defence. Eventually, the British conceded defeat, and the ships were taken to Mauritius, where their cargo of rice and other foodstuffs was seized by the authorities. As it happened, there was a severe food shortage on the island, so Surcouf was feted as a hero.

## DAVID AND GOLIATH

Up to this point, Surcouf's actions at sea had been technically illegal, so he returned to France to receive a letter of marque. This was a document issued by the government that would allow him to attack enemy shipping, under the legal protection of the authorities. With this under his belt, he now became a fully-fledged privateer, a role that he relished. With a new, heavily armed ship, the *Clarisse*, and a crew of over 100 men, he began to roam the seas, capturing ships wherever he went, from Europe to the Far East. On one occasion, he captured a British ship, the *Auspicious*, with a cargo worth thousands, and was forced to speed home with the British navy in hot pursuit.

With continuing hostilities between France and Britain, Surcouf became one of the leading privateers of his day. As captain of the warship *Confiance*, he captured a total of nine British ships, as well as the *Kent*, a ship sailing under charter from the East India Company, which at the time had a monopoly on trade in the area. Once again, it was a David and Goliath situation, with the small French force facing the much larger British one, but Surcouf eventually managed to capture the *Kent*. As a result of this triumph, he returned home covered in glory, and became a household name in France. In Britain, however, he was regarded as a common pirate, and the British government offered a sizeable reward for his capture.

## LEGION D'HONNEUR

At the dawn of the 19th century, Surcouf had a change of heart, retired from privateering, married and settled down in St Malo to attend to his business affairs. By now, he was an extremely wealthy man, and had enriched the city's coffers too. It was rumoured that the Emperor Napoleon himself often borrowed from St Malo's treasury to pay for his war campaigns. Surcouf enjoyed friendly relations with the emperor, and on one occasion asked him if he could build a terrace made of coins outside his residence. The emperor refused, saying he did not want people walking on the image of his face, whereupon Surcouf built the terrace with the coins stacked upright, with the edges as a surface, so that the royal visage would not be sullied.

Yet despite his life of ease in St Malo, Surcouf could not keep away from the sea for long. In 1804, he succumbed to the temptation to return to the battle at sea. Once again, he managed to defeat his enemies, making such a reputation for himself that when opponents heard he was on-board a ship, they often simply surrendered or sailed away. After many adventures, he returned to France and was decorated with the *Legion d'Honneur* by Napoleon.

## FINAL BATTLE

Surcouf's final years were spent as a ship owner, establishing trade in many parts of the world, including the West Indies, Canada, India and Africa. He amassed an enormous amount of wealth, and was generous in financing municipal initiatives of all kinds. His final battle was a small one, but typical of his courage: seeing an old man being bullied by Prussian officers in a bar, he fought them off with a pool cue, defeating all 11 of them.

Surcouf died on 8 July 1827. His passing was marked by a grand funeral cortege of 50 sailing boats, who carried his body to its final resting place out at sea.

LEFT: A painting by Ambroise Louis Garneray, depicting Robert Surcouf and his crew taking the *Kent*, in the Gulf of Bengal, 7 October 1800.

# JOSEPH BARSS

Joseph Barss felt he was born to sail the seven seas, just like his father before him. As the captain of the *Rover* and the *Liverpool Packet*, he took part in adventure after adventure, and lived to become one of Nova Scotia's most famous privateers.

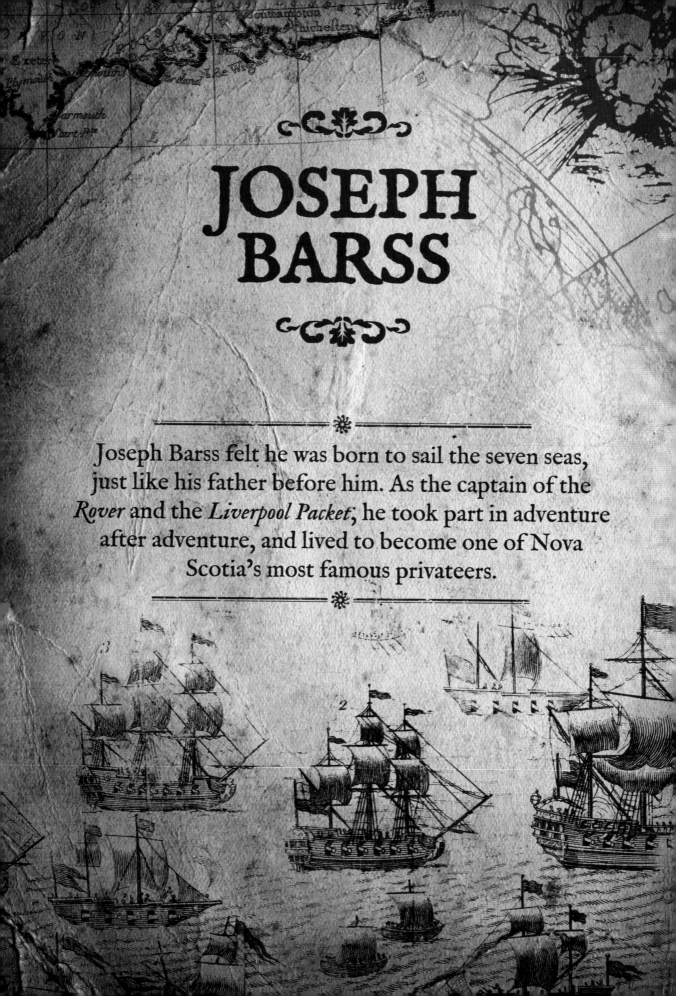

**T**he son of a famous sea captain, Joseph Barss Sr, it is no surprise that the young Joseph had a fascination with ships and in fact anything to do with the ocean. This fascination led to Joseph Barss Jr becoming one of the most famous privateers to come out of Nova Scotia.

The Barss family was one of the first to settle in Liverpool, Nova Scotia, in 1761 and they built one of the largest houses in the area to accommodate their fourteen children. The house still stands today and is part of the Lane's Privateer Inn, with 12 large rooms and an enormous kitchen with a large fireplace and several brick ovens.

Liverpool was a seaside community and its people relied heavily on the ocean to make their living. They built their own sailing vessels using timber from the nearby forest and sailed up and down the American coast, trading as they went. They traded wood and pickled fish in return for rum and salt, and the young Joseph watched with envy each time his father sailed out of port. At the age of 14, Joseph, being one of the older children in the Barss family, was delighted when his father allowed him to become a crew member on his salmon-fishing boat. The young boy took to the sea like a duck to water and, having watched all the privateering activities in and out of the port for the past decade, it is no wonder that he ended up serving on the crew of more than one pirate ship. In 1798, he was appointed second lieutenant on-board the privateer, the *Charles Mary Wentworth* and by October the following year, he was offered the command of the *Lord Spencer*. Unfortunately the schooner sank after hitting a reef in the West Indies, but Barss and his entire crew survived and were picked up by other privateer ships in the area. The United States was at war with France and Barss Sr suffered heavy losses from French war ships and fellow privateers. Barss Sr started to fit out his own ships to attack enemy French and Spanish ships in the Caribbean Sea.

## THE ROVER

Joseph Barrs Jr's fame as a privateer stems from his command of the brig *Rover*, a noted pirate vessel from Liverpool. It was renowned for its voyages under the command of Alexander Godfrey, another privateer to come from the Nova Scotia region. The *Rover* carried a crew of approximately 60 men and there are several entries in the diary of Simeon Perkins, a merchant from Liverpool, giving accounts of the *Rover's* activities.

On the 26 January 1801, the *Rover* departed for sea, with Joseph Barss Jr, as Commander. Eleven weeks later, on 18 April, the *Nostra Sen. Del Carman* hauled into Liverpool, a prize that the *Rover* sent in. Not long after that, on 8 May, the *Rover* returned to Liverpool. She was not left to lie long, for on 11 May, the owners were fitting her out again.

On this occasion (11 May), Joseph Barss Jr turned down the offer of captaining the *Rover*, and spent the next few years on merchant vessels. In 1804, he married Olivia DeWolf, who was the daughter of Elisha DeWolf, a judge and political figure in Nova Scotia. DeWolf represented King's County in the Nova Scotia House of Assembly from 1793 to 1799 and from 1818 to 1820. Joseph and Olivia went to live with Joseph Barss Sr on Dean's Point.

In 1812, the United States declared war on Britain and thousands of privateers were employed to attack British ships in the North Atlantic. Joseph Barss Jr was given the captaincy of a captured slave ship called the *Liverpool Packet*. Originally nicknamed the *Black Joke*, the

*Liverpool Packet* was a slave trader captured by the Royal Navy. She was a Baltimore clipper schooner, 53 ft long with an 18 ft hold. After being refitted the schooner was armed with guns, pistols, muskets, pikes, cutlasses, grappling irons and nets. The new *Liverpool Packet* was given a crew of 140 men from Nova Scotia and, under the command of Joseph Barrs, succeeded in capturing between 100 and 120 ships off New England. Joseph was renowned for his astute command of the vessel and his fair treatment of prisoners. When his bounty was auctioned, it raised an enormous amount of money. By law, when a prize was captured it was sent to the privateer's home port and inspected. It was then sent to Halifax, where a court of vice admiralty would determine whether the vessel and its captain had been captured legally. If the prize was considered legal, a date was set to auction the vessel. If the prize was deemed illegal, it was returned to its owner and a fine would be levied against the privateer who made the capture. It is considered that as many as 50 of Barss' captured vessels were deemed to be legal.

## Barss Meets His Match

In June 1813, the *Liverpool Packet* finally met her match, in the much larger American privateer, the *Thomas* of Portsmouth, New Hampshire. This defeat brought no shame on Joseph Barrs, as the *Liverpool Packet* was completely outnumbered in size, manpower and weapons. After fighting bravely, the *Liverpool Packet* was forced to surrender, but not before several members of the *Thomas* had been killed. Captain Barss was taken to Portsmouth where, manacled and guarded by militia, he was made to march through the streets. After several months of imprisonment, Barss was released on the condition that he did not resume command of any privateer vessel. However, he broke the terms of his parole when, in 1814, he took command of the *Wolverine*. Joseph was captured for a second time and spent another brief spell in prison. At the end of the war, Joseph came back to Liverpool, but his health was suffering as a result of his spells in prison where conditions were poor and rations were sparse.

Joseph and his wife decided to retire away from the ocean and made plans to buy a farm in Kentville, Nova Scotia. However, shortly before their move a thief broke into the family home on Dean's Point and stole a variety of valuables. The thief was an Irishman by the name of Hurley. Joseph was woken up by a noise downstairs and decided to go and investigate. He pursued Hurley to the riverbank and managed to catch him, recovering the majority of the stolen goods. Hurley was sentenced to death by hanging at a trial in Liverpool in July 1817.

That summer the Barss family moved to their farm where they raised a large family of nine children. Joseph Barss died at Oak Grove Farm on 3 August 1824, at the relatively young age of 49. Joseph Barss Sr died two years later and father and son were both buried in the cemetery at Oak Grove, Kentville.

# Women Pirates

# GRACE O'MALLEY

Grace O' Malley was not called 'The Sea Queen of Connaught' for nothing. This formidable woman, who was born into a noble Irish sea-faring family, came to control an entire fleet of ships, five castles and landholdings, and even got away with insulting the most powerful female of the age – Queen Elizabeth I.

In Irish folklore there are stories of a fearsome pirate named Grace O'Malley. She lived in 16th century Ireland and her exploits at sea earned her nicknames such as 'Pirate Queen' and 'The Sea Queen of Connaught'. Her adventures seem like the stuff of fiction, but in fact, Grace O'Malley was a real person, fighting against the social norms of the time to become the most infamous female pirate in Irish history.

Grace O'Malley is known in folklore by many different translations and variations of her name: Granuaile, Gráinne Mhaol, Gráinne Ui Mháille. However it is the anglicized version, Grace O'Malley, that she is most commonly linked to. She was born in County Mayo, Ireland, in 1530 into Irish nobility. Her father was Owen 'Black Oak' O'Malley, legendary sea captain and chieftain of the O'Malley clan, her mother was Margaret and she had a half-brother named Dónal na Piopa, which translates to Donal of the Pipes. They lived on Clare Island, an area which has become synonymous with Grace and her escapades. The O'Malley's were a powerful family, their clan controlling what is now known as the Barony of Murrisk.

## DESTINED TO SAIL

As a child, Grace O'Malley loved nothing more than to sit with her father, listening to his adventures of the high seas and learning from his vast experience of sailing and international trade. Sometimes she would visit his ship, stand firm on the bridge, bark orders at the crew and stare out to sea, dreaming of a sea-faring future. Grace O'Malley was no ordinary child. She knew she was destined to sail. She begged time after time to be allowed to join her father on one of his trading voyages to Spain, but her mother would argue that sailing was a most unbecoming pursuit for a young girl. But Grace was determined. When her mother, hoping to deter her, warned

that her long hair would get tangled in the ropes aboard the ship, she simply cut it all off. Little Grace then put on her brother's clothes and declared herself ready to sail. Her half-brother teased her, cruelly naming her 'Gráinne Mhaol', which translates to 'Bald Grace', but she didn't care. Perhaps endeared by her persistence, her mother gave in and Grace got her first taste of life at sea.

## LEARNING THE ROPES

Grace proved to be a handy crew member. Legend has it that her father told her that if ever the ship were attacked, she should hide below decks. On one occasion, the O'Malley ship was stormed by British pirates. Being a natural rebel she ignored her father's instructions and instead scaled the rigging. This act of defiance ended up saving her father's life. From her unique viewpoint she saw a pirate creeping up behind her father with his dagger raised, in a moment of courage she leapt through the air and landed on the pirate. The noise she made on her descent caused such a distraction that the O'Malley crew quickly took control and won the battle.

In 1546, aged 16, it was arranged that Grace married Dónal an-Chogaidh (Donal of the Battle) O'Flaherty. This union made political sense as Grace was the daughter of a chieftain and O'Flaherty was an heir to the O'Flaherty title, the clan that hoped to eventually rule Iar Connacht. They wed in his castle in Bunowen,

RIGHT: This bronze statue of Grace O' Malley, by artist Michael Cooper, stands in the grounds of Westport House, Ireland.

Connemara. O'Flaherty was from a sea-faring background too and consequently had a fleet of ships. It didn't take long for Grace to assume control of the ships and the surrounding waters. It was highly rare at this time for women to have any power whatsoever, let alone be in charge of an entire fleet of ships, however it was Grace's knowledge of politics, tribal disputes and trading that won her the respect and acceptance she had come to expect. In between her many voyages she managed to make time for a more traditional role, becoming a mother. Between 1547 and 1552 the couple had three children; two sons, Owen and Murrough, and a daughter, Margaret.

In 1560 O'Flaherty died in battle. Around this time Grace and her army of men ran into trouble with rival clan, the Joyces. O'Flaherty had taken a fortress belonging to the Joyce clan and once they learnt of his death they decided to reclaim it. The castle was dubbed 'Cock's Castle' by the Joyces due to Dónal's attitude problem – something he was notorious for. When the siege began at the fortress Grace showed her resourcefulness by allegedly melting lead from the roof and pouring it onto the heads of the attacking soldiers, a move which bizarrely impressed the Joyces. Suffice to say Grace's gang won the battle and the fortress remained under her control, with one difference, the Joyces humbly renamed it 'Hen's Castle'.

## A Career in Piracy

Following her husband's death Grace returned to O'Malley territory, Clare Island, taking with her many O'Flaherty supporters that had become loyal to her. Being a widow she was legally entitled to a portion of her late husband's estate, but for some unknown reason the O'Flahertys were against this and wished to support her at their own discretion. This did not suit Grace one bit. Determined to make her own fortune she took her fleet of ships and an estimated 200 followers to sea and embarked on her career in piracy. From her headquarters she would monitor passing ships and impose a unique tax on anyone daft enough to sail near her shores. Trading ships would often pass by and Grace's ships would surround them, storm abroad and demand money or cargo in return for safe passage. Resistance was futile. Once the tax was paid, Grace's ships would retreat back to their bays and await the next opportunity.

With Clare Island and Clew Bay under Grace's control she effectively became a chieftain of the O'Malley clan. However, there was one castle she wanted to acquire, the nicely concealed Rockfleet. This belonged to Richard-an-Iarainn Burke, known locally as 'Iron Richard' due to the coat of mail he always wore. In 1566 she approached him and they agreed to marry under Brehon Law, this meant that the marriage would only last a year and either party could terminate it when the time was up. And indeed, Grace did just that, according to legend ending the marriage by saying 'I release you' to Richard. By the end of that year she'd taken control of Rockfleet castle and moved her ships and army in. During their short marriage they produced a son, Theobald whom legend would have us believe was delivered on-board a ship minutes before a battle took place, with Grace springing into action shortly after giving birth. Her attacks on ships, islands and even fortresses across shorelines continued for the next 20 years, her legend becoming more interwoven into Irish history. Grace's piracy empire continued to grow, besides the fleets of ships, five castles and landholdings, she also had herds of cattle which was a sure sign of wealth. However, the English were starting to invade Ireland, taking land by force or bribery. Grace could not be tempted by the offer of an English title and rebelled against their invasion.

In 1584 Englishman, Sir Richard Bingham, was appointed governor of Connaught. His first act was to usurp all remaining chieftains and clans and eliminate the power they had amassed. Grace O'Malley was his biggest target. He successfully removed most of her possessions and even sent away her followers, forcing her into poverty. Strangely, he then informed Grace

he wished to call a truce. Upon her arrival at his headquarters he seized her and condemned her to death, luckily she was rescued and managed to flee. A few years passed and Bingham was still set on capturing Grace. In 1586 his troops brutally killed her son, Owen, letting her know she wasn't forgotten. Grace, now in her late 50, returned to her life at sea. Around this time the Spanish Armada was fighting the English around the Scottish and Irish coastlines. It is unknown whether Grace fought alongside the English or was only fighting to protect what little she had left.

By the early 1590s Bingham was still pursuing the 'pirate queen'. The Irish rebellion against the English was growing and naturally Grace would be a huge threat. He cowardly reported her to Queen Elizabeth I for treason, calling her 'the nurse to all rebellions in Ireland', this seemed to have no effect, however. His next move was to get Grace's son, Murrough, to side with him. He then set about trying to seize Grace again, this time at sea. Grace, in her element and still a force to be reckoned with, fought back and seized an English ship. In 1592 she wrote a letter to Queen Elizabeth I and demanded she acknowledge the injustices perpetrated by Bingham, however this was ignored by the monarch.

In 1593 Bingham captured Theobald and Grace's half-brother and charged them with treason. This was the final straw. With their lives on the line she made a decision of historical significance. She decided to travel to London and demanded an audience with the queen. The journey was dangerous, with numerous English ships plaguing the sea, but Grace's expertise got her safely to shore. It is not known why Queen Elizabeth agreed to meet with Grace, perhaps she was intrigued by this fierce female warrior. It is written that during their meeting Grace sneezed, and a courtier politely handed her an expensive lace handkerchief, she then wiped her nose and threw it in the fireplace. Queen Elizabeth scolded her, exclaiming the handkerchief was a gift and should have been put in her pocket after use, Grace argued she would not keep a soiled handkerchief, implying she was far cleaner than the queen. This was met with silence, and then suddenly the queen roared with laughter. After this, Queen Elizabeth ordered the release of Grace's family and the return of her possessions.

Grace O'Malley sailed triumphantly back to Ireland and to her life of piracy. She died in 1603 at Rockfleet castle, aged 73 years old.

Rockfleet Castle, in Clew Bay,
Co Mayo, Ireland.

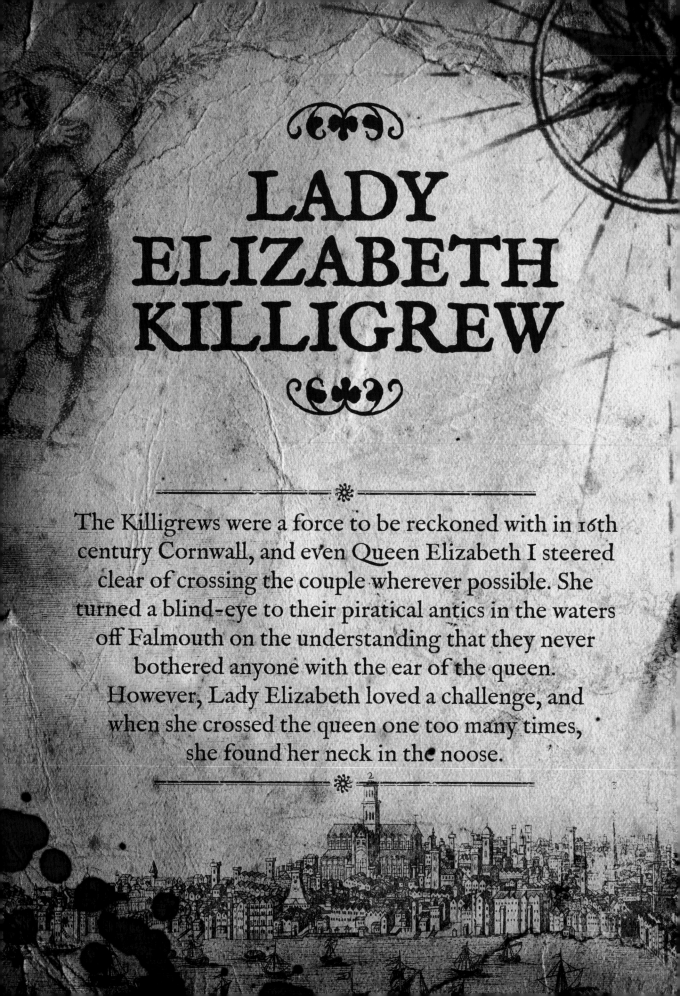

# LADY ELIZABETH KILLIGREW

The Killigrews were a force to be reckoned with in 16th century Cornwall, and even Queen Elizabeth I steered clear of crossing the couple wherever possible. She turned a blind-eye to their piratical antics in the waters off Falmouth on the understanding that they never bothered anyone with the ear of the queen. However, Lady Elizabeth loved a challenge, and when she crossed the queen one too many times, she found her neck in the noose.

In late 16th century Cornwall, England, lived Sir John and Lady Elizabeth Killigrew. Being members of the English aristocracy the Killigrews were naturally very rich, but their fortune was not necessarily comprised of family heirlooms and landholdings. In fact, the Killigrews were also pirates, using their unique coastal setting to operate as outlaws. Unusually it wasn't Sir John that afforded the name Killigrew a place in pirate history, but it was his wife, Elizabeth. The legend of Lady Killigrew has been muddled somewhat over time, she is referred to as 'Mary' as much as 'Elizabeth'. One things for certain, Lady Killigrew was an aristocrat with a rather unladylike difference.

Sir John and Lady Elizabeth lived in Arwenack House, overlooking Falmouth Harbour. From here Sir John controlled whole fleets of pirates. He had been given numerous royal titles over the years, and although piracy was illegal, the authorities turned a blind eye if bribed appropriately, especially where nobility were concerned. There was also an unspoken agreement with Queen Elizabeth I, if the Killigrews did not target her or her associates, and could be relied on as privateers in a war situation, they could carry on their business. This suited everyone, apart from their victims. The Killigrews lived a lavish lifestyle and used their dodgy dealings to support it. Lady Elizabeth was the daughter of a pirate and so had grown up in the trade. She knew how to sail and wasn't afraid to play rough, legend has it she enjoyed piracy more than her husband.

In 1581 a Spanish ship, *Marie of San Sebastián*, was caught in a tempestuous gale. The crew managed to navigate the ship to Falmouth harbour to take refuge. Seeing the battered-looking ship, the Killigrews rushed out to see if they could help. The captain and his first mate were offered a room at the castle and Lady Elizabeth spoilt them with her hospitality. They became so comfortable enjoying the decadence of the castle that they decided to stay a few days

longer, after all, the gale was still raging so sailing would have been very dangerous. What they didn't realize, was that while they were relaxing, Lady Elizabeth was using various opportunities to assess the ship and work out whether it was worth looting. Unfortunately for the Spaniards, it was.

## LOOTING THE MARIE OF SAN SEBASTIAN

One night, while her guests were enjoying the company of Sir John, Lady Elizabeth excused herself. She went and changed out of her expensive clothes and put on something less special. She then rounded up Arwenack House's staff, which doubled as her pirate crew. She led them down the secret tunnel that connected the house to a concealed spot on the shore. Here, they climbed into rowing boats and surrounded the ship. Since the gale was causing so much noise, the pirates were able to climb aboard undetected. Lady Elizabeth's men stormed the decks and quickly killed all the Spanish crew, throwing their bloody corpses overboard. The pirates then went about emptying the ship of its cargo, and loading their rowing boats with treasure. Once they'd taken all the valuables, Lady Elizabeth rowed back to shore and crept back through the secret

RIGHT: Falmouth Harbour, by JMW Turner

passageway. Once home she put on her expensive clothes again, and rejoined her husband and guests. In the meantime, her pirates were busy sailing the ship out of sight and sinking it, then sailing back to the castle. This operation took less than two hours.

The next day the weather had subsided and their guests decided it was time to head back out to sea. Walking down to the docks they were shocked to discover their ship had disappeared. Initially the Spaniards were suspicious of the Killigrews. Many were sure Lady Elizabeth was guilty, but without any evidence nothing could be proved. When this incident was reported, Queen Elizabeth I decided to overlook it. This was a close call for Lady Elizabeth, the queen would not be able to ignore another high-profile act of piracy.

In 1582 a similar circumstance occurred. A German merchant ship anchored at Falmouth harbour. Lady Elizabeth knew it to be full of

gold, silver and jewels. She could not resist. Selecting a small crew of her best pirates, they rowed up to the ship as they had before, killed all that were on-board and stole the contents. It can be assumed that Lady Elizabeth thought she'd be let off this crime of greed and murder, but what she didn't know was that the German ship had close ties with Queen Elizabeth I, and when word reached her, she was furious. She immediately ordered the apprehension and execution of Lady Elizabeth and two of her pirates. As the date of Lady Elizabeth's hanging approached the queen suddenly pardoned her, and instead sentenced her to a long prison term. It is unknown why the queen changed her mind. It is most widely assumed that despite her powerful position, the Killigrew clan were not a family one particularly wanted to cross. Lady Elizabeth was eventually released from prison and rejoined Sir John at Arwenack House. Whether they lived out their final years as pirates is unknown.

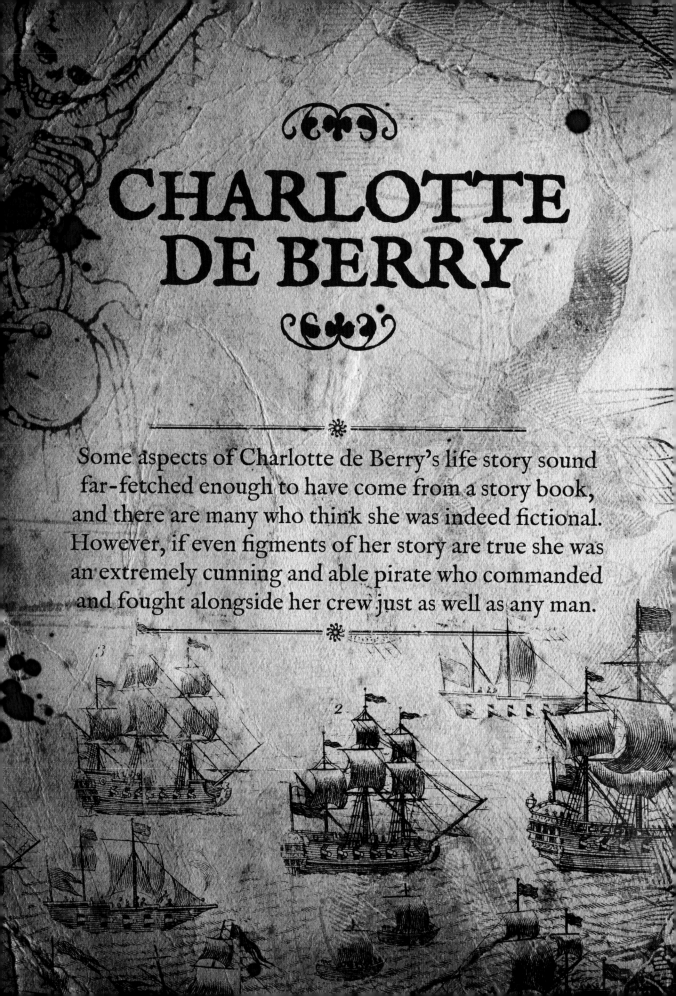

# CHARLOTTE DE BERRY

Some aspects of Charlotte de Berry's life story sound far-fetched enough to have come from a story book, and there are many who think she was indeed fictional. However, if even figments of her story are true she was an extremely cunning and able pirate who commanded and fought alongside her crew just as well as any man.

harlotte de Berry is thought to have been born in England in 1636. However not much is documented about her until exactly two centuries later when she appeared in an 1836 'penny dreadful' written by Edward Lloyd entitled *History of the Pirates*. Because of this she is widely regarded as being fictional. Most reports of her life seem to stem from the writings of Lloyd, however, there are a few variations to her legend in the public domain.

Edward Lloyd's story begins when Charlotte was in her mid-to-late teens living in a coastal town. Her father was retired from his sea-faring life by this time and as Charlotte inherited his keen interest and almost romantic fascination with the sea, he would share his knowledge with her. She would speak of wishing she'd been born male so she could pursue a sailor's life, these feelings sometimes drove her to dress in men's clothes and visit public houses near the docks, where she knew sailors would be. There was always a risk of her real identity being discovered but Charlotte could quite easily disguise her female shape under a baggy shirt and jacket. Luckily most sailors had long hair which they tied back, so she did just that. She would sit and drink with the men, discussing all things nautical, her knowledge was so great that her façade was never uncovered. On one occasion she met a sailor named Jack Jib, an experienced seaman with over 20 years of sailing under his belt. They took an instant liking to each other and married – it is assumed she revealed her true identity quite early on. Jack got called up by the Royal Navy to go to sea, and she was determined to join him. Charlotte again donned men's clothes and got accepted, as a male sailor, to join Jack at sea. They fought alongside each other in six battles and she saved his life four times, her reputation as a great warrior growing with every victory. Their affection towards each other was noted by other sailors on-board, but never was the nature of their relationship questioned.

However, things were about to change. Jack was suddenly accused of numerous crimes by a tyrannical lieutenant. He was brought before a court martial and sentenced to be flogged through the fleet. This most horrific of treatments left Jack in an awful state and he only survived the injuries for a further week before his body shut down completely. Charlotte was inconsolable and at this point something inside her changed, she swore revenge on the man responsible for prescribing this punishment.

When the ship docked up and the crew were paid, everyone disbanded. Charlotte kept an eye on the movements of the dastardly lieutenant. She waited patiently in a lane where she knew he would be passing. Then, choosing her moment carefully, she sprung from the shadows and shot him dead with her pistol. Then, like the pirate she was, plundered his pockets and stole all his gold coins.

## FORCED MARRIAGE

Some time passed and Charlotte remained on land. She began working in a waterfront saloon as an 'entertainer'. A sea merchant named Captain Wilmington took a shine to her and repeatedly requested her company, Charlotte refused again and again. He finally gave up asking nicely and simply kidnapped her, forced her to marry him and took her aboard his ship bound for Africa. Wilmington was a nasty man with a filthy temper. He would order the punishment of his crew on the slightest of offences and secretly they

all began to plot against him. On many occasions Charlotte would intervene and convince her husband not to administer cruel beatings, making her increasingly popular. She began to hear rumours of the crews desires to dispatch Wilmington, and was waiting for an opportunity to offer her services. One day the ship moored up on an island and the seven crew members disembarked. Charlotte convinced Wilmington to allow her to follow and so she did, keeping a distance away so the crew did not know she was eavesdropping. The sailors discussed their deadly plan to kill Wilmington but could not decide who would lead the mutiny.

At this moment, Charlotte appeared before them and one of the sailors drew his cutlass and exclaimed, 'We are betrayed!'. Before he could lunge at her she said, 'Hold! I am your friend, alike the enemy of Captain Wilmington, and burning for revenge. I have overheard all you have said, and only swear to be faithful to me, and I will rid you of your cares, and place the vessel in your hands this very night.' The sailors were in complete shock, but as Charlotte told them of her years at sea and all the bloody battles she had attended dressed in men's clothing, their shock turned to raucous applause. They agreed to follow her and do as she instructed. The sailors returned to the ship with the supplies they'd been sent for, and shortly after Charlotte arrived back. Captain Wilmington suspected nothing.

Charlotte and Wilmington went to bed as normal. She lay next to him and waited until she was sure he was in a deep sleep. She then retrieved the knife she had hidden earlier, and plunged it down onto his neck, almost

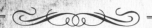

disconnecting his head from his body entirely. She then sounded a signal to the crew to alert them that the deed was done, and they came running into the cabin and marvelled at her bravery. A couple of the crew weren't comfortable with murder and mutiny but they were tossed overboard which eliminated that problem. Charlotte now had complete control of the vessel and her crew rejoiced, shouting 'Long life and success to the gallant female pirate captain, Charlotte de Berry!'. And so began Charlotte's career as a pirate captain.

## CAPTAIN RODOLPH

Charlotte once again began dressing in men's clothing, even giving herself a masculine pseudonym, Captain Rodolph. Rumours of Captain Rodolph's crew and their cruel capabilities spread round Africa's coast. They cruised the seas looking for vessels that traded in gold dust. They would storm the ships, take all their findings and from the crew try and recruit more pirates. If they were met with any resistance they would kill them. On one of their regular patrols they encountered an English vessel named *Lizard*. As it approached Charlotte could see how well equipped it was, and judging by the size of the vessel, safely assumed there would be valuable cargo on-board. She resolved to attack it and take the ship by force. She hoisted the black flag which was met with laughter from her opposition. The battle commenced and both sides fought with equal ferocity and determination. Charlotte's crew boarded the *Lizard* three times only to be driven back; they had clearly met their match. The ships were getting blown to pieces and

the decks were strewn with slain pirates, but Charlotte persisted with her pistol, shooting down the *Lizard's* captain. The remaining crew were intimidated by Charlotte's prowess but vowed to regain control of their ship. In the bloody chaos of the battle most of the sailors were thrown overboard and as they clambered back aboard dodging the hail of bullets, the *Lizard* began to sink and quickly disappeared beneath the sea taking with her the remaining crew and the treasure. Charlotte was disappointed to have lost so many men and the *Lizard's* treasure, but she soon set about repairing her own ship, known as the *Trader*, and recruiting more sailors.

Back on land Charlotte removed her male attire and dressed in women's clothes. While preparing for their next voyage Charlotte met a wealthy 22 year-old who fell hopelessly in love with her. He immediately proposed and Charlotte was so taken with him that they married in secret. She then revealed to him her occupation and told him he was welcome to join her as an outlaw at sea. He realized he could not be without her and agreed to join the crew, bringing with him a whole posse of his father's slaves to man the decks.

## CANNIBALISM

Three years of piracy passed when one day the *Trader* was hit by a tempest, so violent was the storm that some of the crew were flung overboard along with food provisions. Following three days of starvation the remaining crew reached breaking point and came to a most gruesome decision – they would draw straws to determine who would sacrifice their lives for the good of their comrades. The shortest straw drawn was that of Charlotte's husband. Charlotte immediately implored them to take her life instead. Remarkably one of his slaves intervened and begged, out of loyalty, to take his place. Before this could even be discussed the slave took his own life with a dagger and they feasted on his

flesh for the next two days. It was then time to draw straws again. Unbelievably, the same thing happened, another slave offered himself up in place of his master. Two days later, Charlotte's husband, obviously incredibly unlucky, drew the shortest straw for the third time. Charlotte pleaded with the crew to wait a little while longer in hope of rescue, but they were ravenous, and so they took the flesh from his calves. Charlotte begged for them to keep him alive one more day, sure that help would arrive, but they refused and said they would kill her too.

Charlotte's husband knew his fate was sealed and asked they shoot him and be convinced that he was utterly dead before they finish hacking him up. They agreed and shot him, however, his heart had barely stopped beating before the greedy pirates devoured him. One of the sailors cruelly offered her a portion of her husband which drove her to run to another side of the ship where she screamed in distress. Suddenly she heard a sailor exclaiming, 'a sail! a sail!'. Help had arrived.

Soon after their rescue Charlotte's crew were involved in one final battle. By this time the grotesque manner in which she lost her husband, and the knowledge that his death could have been prevented if the crew had waited for help, had driven her insane. She ambled madly about the ship, pistols in both hands, as the battle raged around her. She received a fatal blow from a rival pirate's cutlass, and as she was tossed overboard she was heard to exclaim, 'My husband! Thy bride, Charlotte, the female pirate, comes to join thee!'.

# CHING SHIH

---

Ching Shih was the most powerful pirate queen of them all. Upon her husband's death she took control of the Red Flag Fleet, a pirate federation made up of 70,000 men, whom she ruled with an iron fist, not a bad career move for a low-born former prostitute from Canton.

---

Ching Shih was the most feared female pirate of her time. With her tens of thousands of pirate crew and hundreds of vessels under her control she terrorized the Chinese coast; plundering, pillaging, slaughtering, abducting, extorting, and mainly, beheading. The ruthlessness of her federation was notorious and her ever-increasing power and influence infuriated the Chinese government. After a few years and numerous failed attempts to defeat her, they negotiated an amnesty and she lost all her men and vessels. However, Ching Shih wasn't prepared to lose everything she'd worked so hard for, she demanded to keep her loot.

Shih Yang was born in 1775. There is little recorded about her until she became a prostitute on a floating brothel in Canton, north of Hong Kong in 1801. It was there that she met a patron of the brothel, Zheng Yi, and soon they were married; her name changed accordingly to 'Zheng Yi Sao', meaning 'wife of Zheng Yi'. Zheng Yi was a major player in piracy, he was a member of an infamous family of pirates that had been in operation since the 17th century. When Shih Yang entered his family she was offered a route out of prostitution and into piracy, but not as any old outlaw, but alongside one of the most powerful men at sea. Zheng Yi worked hard to expand his empire. By 1804 he used his reputation and military expertise to gather a coalition comprised of competing Cantonese pirates. This formed the largest pirate fleet in China, known as the 'Red Flag Fleet'. They commanded 50,000 pirates which is a staggering number compared to the 5,000 – 6,000 pirates known to exist in the Caribbean sea during the same period in history. Female pirates were not uncommon in Chinese waters and Zheng Yi Sao proved herself to be a great warrior.

## WIDOWED AT SEA

In 1807 Zheng Yi was killed during a particularly violent gale, leaving Zheng Yi Sao a widow.

She then became 'Ching Shih' meaning 'widow of Zheng Yi', the name she is most commonly affiliated with. It was unusual for women to be in positions of power but Ching Shih saw his death as an opportunity to manoeuvre herself into leadership and quickly assumed control of their ever-growing empire. Ching Shih ran a tight ship, literally. By now the number of pirates under her command reached 70,000 and any that broke her rules could be eliminated and replaced with ease. One of her rules on-board was that if any pirates raped a female captive then they would be beheaded. From this one could assume Ching Shih was a pioneer for women's rights, but the truth was the female was also killed. Consensual sex was banned too, with the male offender being beheaded and the female having weights attached to her ankles and thrown overboard. Ching Shih was deeply concerned with the attractiveness of her captives. Women deemed 'ugly' were set free whereas beautiful women were kept and allowed to be purchased by her pirates. Once a purchase was made, this couple were seen as 'married'. If the pirate cheated on his wife, he would be decapitated. If a pirate took loot from the haul, or took unauthorized shore leave, a simple beheading seemed to do the trick. She reserved a rather gruesome punishment for deserters. They would be found and their ears sliced off – a painful penalty but at least they were allowed to

keep their heads. Ching Shih had 1,500 vessels in her empire now, and she handed over the naval operations to Chang Pao, Zheng Yi's adopted son, allowing her to take care of the company finances. Chang Pao became Ching Shih's lover and eventually her husband, despite the fact that at one point she was technically his adopted mother.

## BUSINESS IS BOOMING

Southeast Asia was used to suffering at the hands of Ching Shih. Her fleets targeted fishing villages, markets, towns and cities, levying taxes and stealing goods. The pirates would invade the coastal villages and terrorize the inhabitants, slaughtering anyone who got in their way. They would abduct women and children and sell them into slavery or hold them to ransom. Ching Shih made a fortune extorting money from salt merchants, and even dabbled in the dealing of opium. Her federation offered a 'protection fee' to ships leaving Canton port. This meant the sailors were protected from attack. Of course, this attack would most likely come from Ching Shih's cronies so it was a win-win situation for her. It seemed for a long time that she was getting away with whatever she liked, the Chinese government were sick of it. They repeatedly tried to defeat Ching Shih at sea but these attempts were often met with her simply taking their ships too, only serving to strengthen her business further. By

1808 they had lost 63 ships to the pirate fleet. Problems started to arise in the coalition when there were arguments between squadrons and threats from rival fleets began to increase too.

## A DEAL IS STRUCK

In 1810 the Imperial government secured assistance from British and Portuguese warships but before battle commenced an amnesty was offered to Ching Shih, in return for her resignation from piracy. Ching Shih demanded she could keep her loot, she also negotiated pardons for most of her men and only 126 were executed and 250 received some other form of punishment. The remaining men were offered jobs within the army and Chang Pao was given the role of lieutenant.

Ching Shih and Chang Pao settled in Fukien where they had a son. In 1822 Chang Pao died aged 36, having achieved the rank of colonel. Ching Shih moved back to Guangzhou, Canton and opened a brothel and a gambling house. She died aged 69, a very wealthy woman and a most notorious pirate. In 2007 a character named 'Mistress Ching' appeared in the film *Pirates of the Caribbean: At World's End*. Although it is not confirmed it seems likely that this character, one of the nine pirate lords, is based on Ching Shih, thus securing her legend a place in popular culture.

# Modern Piracy

**P**iracy is a crime most of us associate with romantic novels, children's picture books and multi-million dollar movies. Certainly, in the West piracy is predominantly a thing of the past, the US navy and the US coastguard have eradicated it from US waters and in the Caribbean Sea. No more do seafaring vagabonds roam our oceans in search of ships to capture and loot. However, this is definitely not the case in some other parts of the world, and in those places where piracy is a problem, it appears to be on the increase.

### PIRACY WORLDWIDE

Like other types of property crime, modern piracy tends to occur most in areas of major political unrest and lawlessness where poverty has driven a population to commit extreme criminal acts. It is a serious problem in places such as the Red Sea, in the waters off the Somalian coast and in the Strait of Malacca near Sumatra. These waters are some of the busiest in the world. Over 50,000 vessels pass through them annually, many carrying millions of dollars worth of goods. Consequently the crimes these pirates commit are expensive – piracy is currently estimated to cost the global economy between US $13 and $16 billion dollars a year.

Modern pirates tend to favour small powerful motorboats and dhows, which can be easily hidden or disguised, rather than the large cumbersome vessels of yesteryear. They require less man-power than their predecessors because the crews of most merchant vessels have been vastly reduced to the point where a huge oil tanker may be staffed by only 25 crew members – making them very easy to board and hijack using only a handful of hardened assailants. Weapons are also more sophisticated in the 21st century, today's pirates

LEFT: An Indonesian-made naval patrol boat is seen through a gun site in Jakarta's bay.

routinely carry an array of terrifying and deadly weapons, including assault rifles, shotguns, pistols, mounted machine guns, even rocket-propelled grenades and grenade launchers – quite a departure from the cutlasses and cannons of the 18th century and more than enough to overwhelm the average tanker crew.

## PIRACY AND TERRORISM

Sea robbery and hijacking for ransom are key ways for global terrorists to make money whilst simultaneously drawing widespread attention, however negative, to their plight. These same methods have been utilized for as long as human beings have travelled by sea, they were in constant use by privateers during the 16th, 17th and 18th centuries, and so far the recent war on terror has not successfully combated it. Whilst the majority of pirates belong to organized crime syndicates comprising of corrupt officials, port workers, hired thugs and businessmen who dispose of the loot, the line has been blurred to include some international terrorists whose primary aim is terrorism. The Palestinian Liberation Front (PLF), the IRA and Jemaah Islamiyah – the al Qaeda-linked Indonesian terrorist group, are all known to have attacked shipping as part of their campaign of terror.

## THE ACHILLE LAURO – POLITICAL PIRACY

After a long period of relative silence, piracy once again resurfaced in international news in October 1985, with the high-profile hijacking of the MS *Achille Lauro*, an Italian cruise ship operating out of Naples. On 7 October 1985 she was attacked by four members of the Palestinian Liberation Front (PLF), as she sailed from Alexandria to Port Said, Egypt. The pirates quickly overwhelmed the vessel and took all 100 elderly passengers hostage before demanding the release of 50 Palestinian prisoners. At some point

during the course of their occupation they shot and killed a disabled Jewish-American passenger, 69-year-old Leon Klinghoffer, before throwing his body and his wheelchair overboard. His corpse washed ashore weeks later.

Following a two-day standoff, the Egyptian government (who were apparently unaware of Klinghoffer's murder) granted the hijackers safe passage in exchange for securing the freedom of the ship and her passengers. However, on discovering the murder, US Navy F-14 fighters intercepted the Egyptian airliner flying the terrorists to safety and forced it to land in Sicily, where they were arrested, tried, convicted and sentenced to 30 years behind bars. The group's mastermind, Abu Abbas, was tried in absentia but never served any time in jail for the crime. He later claimed that Klinghoffer had provoked his killers into shooting him by inciting the other passengers. Abbas died in US custody having been captured in Iraq in 2004, following the US invasion.

## THE STRAIT OF MALACCA

The Strait of Malacca is a narrow, 550-mile (900km) long sea-lane between West Malaysia and the Indonesian island of Sumatra. From an economic and strategic point of view this relatively small stretch of water is the most important shipping lane in the world: It is the main channel between the Indian Ocean and the Pacific and the sole route for all Middle Eastern oil bound for China and Japan, and therefore it is a prime stretch of real estate for pirates, who regularly plunder the ships that attempt to pass through it. Piracy in this part of the world is not only a lucrative source of income, but also an important political tool. Historically, the region's rulers have relied on piracy in the strait to help them maintain control, this route was vital to the spice trade during the 18th and 19th centuries, and today oil has simply replaced spice as the product that drives the world economy.

In addition to robbing merchant vessels of their valuable cargo, pirates in the Malacca Straits also tend to kidnap crew members for ransom. Most of the pirates in this region come from Indonesia, where the rule of law is extremely weak. Some of the pirates are sea robbers, but some are terrorists from the Free Aceh Movement, aiming to put pressure on their governments, or to make money to fund the movement by attacking shipping.

## THE NAGASAKI SPIRIT

At 23.20pm on 19 September 1992, the hijacked tanker *Nagasaki Spirit* collided with a container ship named the *Ocean Blessing*. Pirates had boarded the *Nagasaki Spirit* at the northern end of the Malacca Strait and removed its captain from command before setting the ship on autopilot and leaving with their hostage, the ship's master, who they intended to ransom. The *Nagasaki Spirit*, having been left with nobody at the wheel, careered into the *Ocean Blessing*, taking the lives of everyone aboard the *Blessing* and all but two sailors aboard the hijacked ship. The fire on the *Blessing* burned for an incredible six weeks.

## THE PORT OF EYL – A MODERN PIRATE HAVEN

The port of Eyl, in the lawless region of Puntland, Somalia, has become a global centre for piracy in recent years. More than 100 ships were attacked in 2008, over 40 were successfully hijacked and approximately 200 crew members were held for ransom. During their incarceration the majority of these hostages were cared for by the inhabitants of Eyl, indeed the entire town's economy is built around it, and although the actual number of pirates who take part in attacks is relatively small, the townspeople all rely on this booming industry in order to feed their families. Visitors to the town have reported that, as soon as a ship is captured and boarded, people arrive in Eyl wearing smart suits and ties and carrying laptops, each claiming to be the pirates' accountant, or their negotiator etc. It is in this way that the town manages to survive, and even prosper, in an area that is so lawless, corrupt and destitute that the people have few other options besides crime.

ABOVE: An ariel view of Djibouti sea port in the Gulf of Aden.

## Puntland Privateers?

It has been suggested that some members of the Puntland administration maintain secret links with the pirates of Eyl and sanction their behaviour on the high seas, thus echoing the relationships forged between British monarchs and privateers of the 16th and 17th centuries. Ultimately men like Sir Francis Drake had the same aims as these Somali pirates, to get rich quick and bring back a portion of the spoils for their fellow countrymen. These Somali pirates may not be as whimsically dressed as Drake, Newport or Modyford, they sail upon speedboats rather than sloops and carry Kalashnikovs, not cutlasses. But their methods are, on the whole, less violent than their British predecessors, many of whom have gone down in history as gentlemen explorers, and even heroes of their age.

## The Eyl Method

The pirates of Eyl are exceptionally good at what they do. Their sophisticated operations use cutting-edge technology such as GPS and satellite phones, not to mention highly efficient weapons including rocket-propelled grenades and AK47s. The pirates are known to receive tip-offs from contacts in the Gulf of Aden, in the Arabian Sea, but it is not known exactly who these mysterious contacts are, or who they work for. They travel on speedboats with highly powerful outboard motors to reach their targets, and are sometimes launched from much larger vessels, or 'mother ships' further out to sea.

As the speedboat approaches the victim vessel the pirates sometimes fire at the ship in order to scare it into stopping, making it easier to board. Next, they use grappling hooks and irons, some

ABOVE: French luxury yacht *Le Ponant*, which was hijacked by pirates off the coast of Eyl, Puntland, Somalia.

of which are rocket-propelled, to get a hold on the ship before climbing aboard using ropes and ladders. The ship is hijacked and taken into port, the crew become hostages and a ransom message is posted. In contrast with captives of the 16th and 17th centuries, they will be relatively well treated until the ransom has been paid. The going rate for ransom payments is somewhere between US $300,000 and $1.5 million (GBP £168,000 and £838,000), though this clearly depends on the value of the ship, the cargo and the crew. Sometimes, as with the case of the *Sirius Star*, they command a much higher price.

## SIRIUS STAR – THE BIGGEST HIJACK IN HISTORY

The *Sirius Star* is a super tanker owned by Vela International Marine, a Dubai-based company that also owns another 22 oil tankers, each worth somewhere in the region of US$150 million (GBP£100 million). The *Sirius Star* is a massive 1,090ft (332m) long, three times the size of a US navy aircraft carrier and has a capacity of 2.2 million barrels of crude oil, worth an estimated $100 million (£67 million). This number of barrels equates to over 25 per cent of Saudi Arabia's daily output of oil. But, crucially, she is staffed by a crew of just 25 men.

ABOVE: The super tanker *Sirius Star*.

On 15 November 2008, this fully loaded tanker was making its way from Saudi Arabia to the United States, via the Cape of Good Hope, when it became the largest and most valuable vessel ever to be captured by pirates. On 17 November the US navy announced to the world's media that the *Sirius Star* had been captured by pirates about 450 nautical miles (520 miles, or 830 km) south-east of Mombasa, Kenya. For the Pirates of Eyl to have reached the *Sirius Star* from such a distance away, they must have been travelling south at high-speed for three or even four days.

The pirates took the ship nearer to port, and on 19 November a man identified as one of the heist's masterminds, Farah Abd Jameh, made a statement on an audio tape, broadcast by al-Jazeera television, demanding that an undisclosed sum of money be delivered to the oil tanker, where it would be counted by a machine that could detect counterfeit notes. He also remarked that the crew, which consisted of 19 Filipinos, two Britons, two Poles, one Croat and one Saudi Arabian, were being well-treated in accordance with rules governing the treatment of prisoners of war, that they had been allowed to contact their families, that they slept in their usual beds and that the only thing they were missing was their freedom. Marek Nishky, the ship's captain, was able to confirm this for the BBC, albeit under the scrutiny of his guards. He said the crew were safe and in good shape – if a little bored. He also said that he was not aware of any ransom negotiations taking place. It seemed as if the pirates and their hostages could be in for a wait.

On 20 November the pirates issued another demand, this time stipulating a ransom of US$25 million (GBP£16.7 million), and giving Vela just 10 days to pay up or face disastrous consequences. When this was not paid, rather than begin killing the hostages, a crime rarely committed in these waters, the pirates simply reduced their asking price to US$15 million (GBP£10 million).

In an interesting twist, the hostage-takers found themselves the target of a small faction of Somali Islamic militants, who planned to attack the vessel in retaliation for their seizure of a 'Muslim' vessel. Locals in the port reported that this threat forced the pirates to remain offshore whilst negotiations were taking place, and may even have played a part in bringing proceedings to an eventual halt.

On 9 January 2009, after a long and agonizing wait, the *Sirius Star* was freed by the pirates following receipt of a US$3 million (GBP£1.97 million) ransom payment, which was dropped in by parachute. The BBC later reported that five of the fleeing pirates drowned with their share of the loot when their small boat capsized in a storm off the coast of Somalia. The body of one of the pirates later washed ashore, along with US$153,000 (GBP£100,000) in cash, which had been hastily stashed in a plastic bag. Later, one of the pirates, calling himself Deybad, told reporters that they had no intention of harming the crew. He blamed the recent spate of pirate attacks on the lack of peace in Somalia, and the plunder of its waters by foreign fishing trawlers.

## Unstoppable?

Warships from several countries now patrol the Indian Ocean in an attempt to protect what are, after all, some of the world's busiest shipping lanes. Unfortunately though, this form of intervention does not seem to have deterred the pirates at all, in fact they seem prepared to venture further and further out into open water in order to capture and hijack ships, and their targets seem to be growing ever more ambitious. The area targeted by pirates now totals over 25 per cent of the Indian Ocean, making it impossible to police effectively. Most merchant vessels and tankers choose to traverse these waters via a guarded corridor, and there have been no hijackings within these boundaries since it was set up in August 2008, but those ships that venture out of these waters are extremely vulnerable to attack.

# PIRATES IN POPULAR CULTURE

## TREASURE ISLAND – THE BEGINNING OF A PHENOMENON

Of all the creative works to have affected our perception of pirates and piracy, *Treasure Island*, the children's classic written by Robert Louis Stevenson, is the most important. It could even be claimed that all other pirates in popular culture, from Errol Flynn's Captain Blood to Johnny Depp's Captain Jack Sparrow, have more in common with the characters he created than with their real-life counterparts. Indeed the ubiquitous treasure map marked with the letter X, widely considered an indispensable item in any pirate's artillery, was in fact borne out of Stevenson's imagination. There is no evidence that such a thing ever existed in real-life.

*Treasure Island* was first published as a book in 1883, but it was originally serialized in the children's magazine *Young Folks*, under the title *The Sea Cook*, or *Treasure Island*, between 1881 and 1882, Stevenson was 30 years old when he began writing it. His Presbyterian family had links with the sea, his father, grandfather and great uncles were lighthouse designers and engineers. As a reluctant student of engineering at the University of Edinburgh, Stevenson's trips to inspect his relatives' work at Orkney and Shetland failed to ignite his interest in joining the family business, but succeeded in inspiring him to write.

It was during his time as a student that Stevenson was introduced to the bohemian set, including such characters as Sidney Colvin, Fanny (Frances Jane) Sitwell, Lesley Stephen and the English poet William Henley. William Henley became a particularly close friend and literary collaborator in the life of the young writer. He was an energetic and talkative man with a wooden leg, leading some to claim that he was the partial model for the character of Long John Silver. Perhaps the alternative, irreligious bohemian lifestyle Stevenson adopted meant he felt some empathy with the sea-faring outlaws of old. He certainly looked something like his pirate protagonists. He chose to wear his hair long, dress in velveteen jackets and he rarely wore conventional evening dress to parties – habits that, combined with his new-found atheism, so shocked his family that they all but disowned him.

Stevenson suffered from ill-health throughout his life. Many of his contemporaries believed he had tuberculosis, and it certainly seems that his complaints were mainly respiratory. Perhaps Stevenson became fixated with romantic adventures on the high seas as a way of accessing, in his imagination, the robust, health-giving properties of sea air. We'll never know, suffice to say that, since its publication, *Treasure Island* has directly and indirectly caused generations of young boys and girls to long for the freedom and drama of life on the ocean wave.

## CELLULOID SEA DOGS – PIRATES ON FILM

Many of our more romantic ideas about piracy during the golden age have actually come from literature, the theatre and, in particular, film. During the early 20th century Hollywood writers developed a habit of basing their stories loosely on real characters, and often kept names the same. Consequently the public's image of genuine pirates such as Henry Morgan, Blackbeard and Anne Bonney have become inseparable from the statuesque frames of actors like the swarthy Laird Cregar, the ultimate Long John Silver – Robert Newton and the smouldering Maureen O'Hara. It is worth noting, however, that real-life pirates would have been nowhere near as glamorous. A seaman's life was a brutal one, when they were not battling each other, sustaining horrific wounds from cutlasses and cannon shot which could easily become infected, they were battling malnutrition and diseases like scurvy and venereal disease. Disfiguring scars, botched amputations and toothlessness were commonplace, and hygiene non-existent.

## ERROL FLYNN

Perhaps the most famous pirate actor ever to grace the silver screen was the dashing Errol Flynn, an Australian-born actor who made his name in buccaneer blockbusters such as *Captain Blood*. It was this film, a 1935 remake of an earlier film of the same title, that caused Flynn to be typecast in the swashbuckling role, and he went on to make many more, including *The Sea Hawk*, *Adventures of Captain Fabian* and *Against All Flags*, opposite actresses like Maureen O' Hara , Olivia de Havilland, Brenda Marshall and Agnes Moorehead.

## IN LIKE FLYNN

In real-life Errol Flynn had a little too much in common with his on-screen pirate persona. A black sheep of the movie industry, he was a notorious drinker and ladies man, who was famous for throwing wild parties and was often in deep trouble with his bosses at Warner Brothers. In 1942, Flynn, then 33, was charged with the statutory rape of two underage girls, Betty Hansen and Peggy Satterlee. But instead of ending his career, as it no doubt would today, the trial simply succeeded in further cementing his reputation as a ladies man, and did nothing to dent his devil-may-care image.

## PIRATES OF THE CARIBBEAN

If one actor has stolen the 'pirate' mantle from Errol Flynn in recent years, it is Johnny Depp, who starred as Captain Jack Sparrow in the swashbuckling Disney film series *Pirates of the Caribbean*. These films have re-ignited public interest in pirates, they contain all the excitement of the 1950s films, and like them, many of the characters are based loosely on real-life pirates.

The character of Captain Hector Barbossa, the captain of the *Black Pearl* portrayed by actor Geoffrey Rush, is based, in name at least, on the Barbarossa brothers, the 15th century Ottoman privateers. It has been widely publicized that Johnny Depp's portrayal of Jack Sparrow was modelled on the character of Rolling Stone, Keith Richards, but other elements – his costume and dandy demeanour – are probably based on a combination of Calico Jack (John Rackham) and Howell Davis, the Welsh pirate who preferred trickery and disguise to duelling. In the third film of the series, *Pirates of the Caribbean: At World's End*, we meet the nine pirate lords. Whilst, in real life, there was no such thing, the characters that make up the pirate lords are recognizable. Mistress Ching, for example, is quite closely based on Ching Shih. A former prostitute and fierce warrior, she commands an enormous Chinese pirate federation and thinks nothing of beheading her opponents. It is also possible to recognize the famous Indian privateer, Kanhoji Angre and Black Caesar amongst the characters in the Brethren Court.

Blackbeard as portrayed by Ian McShane in
*Pirates of the Caribbean On Stranger Tides* (2011).

# GLOSSARY

**Aft end:** The rear end of a ship.

**Ahoy:** A call to attract attention.

**Avast:** A nautical term meaning 'hold fast' or 'stop what you are doing.'

**Ballast:** Heavy items placed in a ship's bottom to help it stay upright.

**Barbary Coast:** The North African coast of the Mediterranean, where Islamic, or Barbary, corsairs often raided European trading ships.

**Beam:** The measurement of a ship at her widest part.

**Belay:** To tie or secure a rope-end.

**Bilge:** The lowest part of the ship. The dirty water that collects here is called bilge water.

**Bilged on her anchor:** A ship pierced by her own anchor.

**Black Jack:** A large drinking cup made of leather and stiffened with tar. Many dockside pubs served drinks in these.

**Black Spot:** A device thought to have been invented by Robert Louis Stevenson in his novel Treasure Island denoting a pirate passing a death sentence against another pirate.

**Boatswain/Bosun:** Supervises the maintenance of the vessel and its supply stores.

**Boom:** A spar used to extend the foot of a sail.

**Bow:** The very front of the ship's helm.

**Bowsprit:** A spar running out from a ship's bow to which the forestays are fastened.

**Break consort:** To dissolve an agreement between two ships.

**Brigantine:** A two-masted vessel with a full square-rigged foremast, a fore-and-aft rigged mainmast and square sails on the main topmast.

**Broadside:** To fire all the cannons on one side of a ship simultaneously.

**Buccaneer:** Pirates who attacked French and Spanish shipping during the 17th century, although the term has come to denote any pirate or unscrupulous adventurer.

**Bumboo:** A drink of watered-down rum flavoured with nutmeg and sugar.

**Captain:** The person in command of a ship. Unlike naval captains, the crew democratically elected most pirate captains, and therefore they could be replaced at any time by a majority vote. For the most part control of the ship was shared with the quartermaster. However, the captain came into his own when the ship was engaged in battle, for it was then that he assumed ultimate control of the ship and her crew.

**Carpenter:** The officer responsible for the maintenance and repair of the wooden hull, the masts and yards, working under the direction of the ship's master and the boatswain.

**Cat-O'-Nine Tails:** A whip made from rope that was unravelled to form nine separate 'tails'. Each tail was knotted at the end to cause extra pain and suffering.

**Chain shot:** A weapon made from two metal balls tied together, often shot from a cannon in order to destroy a ship's rigging, masts and sails.

**Clap in irons:** To be chained up.

**Corsair:** A pirate, especially along the Barbary Coast.

**Coxswain:** Another name for the helmsman, or the officer who steered the ship.

**Crow's Nest:** A viewing platform high up on a mainmast, used as a lookout position.

**Cutlass:** A short sword with a broad blade. Popularly used at sea because it did not accidentally damage rigging.

**Davy Jones' Locker:** A term for death or an idiom meaning 'the bottom of the sea'. Davy Jones was a sea devil, and his locker a mythical place seamen went to when they died.

**Firebrand:** An outspoken troublemaker.

**First mate:** The captain's right hand man.

**For-and-aft rig:** A sailing rig consisting of many sails set along the line of the keel rather than perpendicular to it.

**Foremast:** The mast nearest the bow of the ship.

**Forestay:** A rope or cable reaching from the head of a ship's foremast to the bowsprit, for supporting the foremast.

**Freebooter:** A person who pillages and plunders, especially a pirate.

**Freighter:** A vehicle, especially a ship, used for carrying freight.

**Frigate:** A fast warship armed with between 20 and 30 guns.

**Galleon:** A large, three mast sailing ship with a square rig and two or more decks, used by the Spanish from the 15th to the 17th century.

**Galley:** A large ship powered by oars. Usually manned by slaves, also a term for the ship's kitchen.

**Galliot:** A light, swift galley ship formerly used in the Mediterranean.

**Helm:** The equipment used to steer a ship.

**Helmsman:** The man who steers the ship.

**Jib:** A triangular staysail from the outer end of the jib boom to the top of the foremast or from the top of the bowsprit to the masthead.

**Jolly Roger:** A flag, usually bearing a skull and crossbones, indicating a pirate ship.

**Keel:** A lengthwise timber or steel structure along the base of a ship, on which the framework of the whole hull is built.

**Knights of St John:** A religious/military order operating out of Rhodes, where they held sovereignty. The Knights of St John were charged with defending the Holy Land, and their allegiance was to the pope.

**Libertalia:** A free communalist colony in Madagascar, said to have been founded by pirates under the leadership of Thomas Tew.

**Master gunner:** Responsible for the ship's guns and ammunition.

**Mate:** The apprentice to the ship's gunner.

**Piece of eight:** A Spanish silver coin worth one peso or eight reales. It was sometimes literally cut into eight pieces, 1 piece being worth 1 real.

**Pinnace:** A small boat powered by sails or oars, which is carried aboard a larger vessel.

**Pirate Round:** A shipping route used by Anglo–American pirates during the 17th century. It led from the western Atlantic, round the southern tip of Africa, stopping at Madagascar, and then on to India.

**Poop deck:** The highest deck at the aft end of a large ship.

**Poringer:** A small cup or bowl.

**Powder monkey:** Young men who were forced to perform the most dangerous work on the ship – manning the gun crew. Besides the constant threat of death or maiming, they were harshly treated, rarely paid and unlikely to be promoted to pirate crew.

**Quartermaster:** The officer chosen to represent the interests of the crew, who received an extra share of the booty when it was divided. He oversaw the day-to-day running of the ship and was equal to the captain in many respects, until they were engaged in battle, when the ship's captain had ultimate authority.

**Rigging:** A system of ropes, chains or cables used to help support a ship's masts.

**Roundsmen:** Pirates who followed the Pirate Round.

**Sailing master:** The officer in charge of navigation and the sailing of the ship.

**Sailor:** The backbone of the ship, able to work the rigging and the sails, as well as navigate and steer the ship.

**Sandbars:** A ridge of sand formed in a river or along a coastline by the action of waves or currents.

**Second mate:** The third in command and a watch-keeping officer, customarily the ship's navigator.

**Ship's gunner:** A person responsible for the ship's cannons.

**Ship's surgeon:** Ship's surgeon was a highly valued position, and consequently they were often kidnapped from the crews of captured ships. They were expected to treat colds, fevers and sexual diseases as well as amputate the limbs of those injured in battle. If the surgeon was kidnapped, either the ship's cook or the carpenter would be asked to step in, since the tools of their trades were thought to be similar!

**Sloop:** A single-masted for-and-aft-rigged sailing boat with a single jib.

**The Company of Royal Adventurers into Africa:** A company set up during the 15th century by the Stuarts under Charles II and a group of London Merchants. They were given a monopoly over the English slave trade in Africa.

**Woold:** To wrap or wind

**Woolding:** A method of torture whereby a string is tied around the victim's eyes and tightened until their eye balls pop out of their sockets.

**Yardarm:** The outer edge of a ship's yard.

**Yard:** A cylindrical spar, tapering to each end, slung across a ship's mast for a sail to hang from.

# INDEX

Inspiring | Educating | Creating | Entertaining

Brimming with creative inspiration, how-to projects, and useful information to enrich your everyday life, Quarto Knows is a favorite destination for those pursuing their interests and passions. Visit our site and dig deeper with our books into your area of interest: Quarto Creates, Quarto Cooks, Quarto Homes, Quarto Lives, Quarto Drives, Quarto Explores, Quarto Gifts, or Quarto Kids.

This edition published in 2017 by Chartwell Books, an imprint of The Quarto Group, 142 West 36th Street, 4th Floor, New York, NY 10018, USA
T (212) 779-4972 F (212) 779-6058
**www.QuartoKnows.com**

Chartwell Books titles are also available at discount for retail, wholesale, promotional, and bulk purchase. For details, contact the Special Sales Manager by email at specialsales@quarto.com or by mail at The Quarto Group, Attn: Special Sales Manager, 401 Second Avenue North, Suite 310, Minneapolis, MN 55401, USA.

10 9 8 7 6 5 4 3 2

ISBN: 978-0-7858-3502-8

Printed in China